SURVIVING SANDY

SURVIVING SANDY

Long Beach Island and the Greatest Storm of the Jersey Shore

SCOTT MAZZELLA

Foreword by Margaret Thomas Buchholz
Introduction by Larry Savadove

Steve Warren, editor

DOWN THE SHORE
PUBLISHING
West Creek, New Jersey

The words "Down The Shore" and the Down The Shore Publishing logos are registered U.S. Trademarks.

Down The Shore Publishing Corp.
Box 100, West Creek, NJ 08092
www.down-the-shore.com

Printed in Canada
10 9 8 7 6 5 4 3

Layout and design by Leslee Ganss
Edited by Steve Warren

Library of Congress CIP Data below refers to the hardcover edition of this book.
Hardcover ISBN 978-1-59322-079-2
Softcover ISBN 978-1-59322-089-1

Library of Congress Cataloging-in-Publication Data

Mazzella, Scott, 1977-
Surving Sandy : Long Beach Island and the greatest storm of the Jersey Shore / Scott Mazzella.
p. cm.
Includes index.
ISBN 978-1-59322-079-2
1. Hurricanes--New Jersey--Long Beach Island. 2. Hurricane damage--New Jersey--Long Beach Island.
3. Hurricanes--New Jersey--Ocean County. 4. Hurricane damage--New Jersey--Ocean County. 5. Hurricane Sandy, 2012. I. Title.
F142.L65M39 2013
974.9'48--dc23
                2013029731

To my wife Liz and my two children, Ryan and Emily, for
weathering the storm with me. I love you.

Contents

Foreword

As long as people live by the sea, they live with the threat of destructive storms — and now, with a record number of people crowded along the shore, plus the gradual sea level rise heightened since the Industrial Revolution, even more so. I recently saw a photograph of downtown Beach Haven under water. At first glance I thought it was 1962, or 1944, but as I looked at the storefronts more closely and the old coupe with water covering the running board, I realized it was taken during the 1938 hurricane. It could almost have been October 30, 2012. But with Superstorm Sandy, four feet of water inundated Beach Haven instead of two feet.

These earlier storms, especially the 1962 northeaster, documented in *Great Storms of the Jersey Shore*, cast a long shadow as Scott Mazzella documents this "Greatest Storm" from its birth in Africa as a tropical depression, through its trail of havoc in the Caribbean, to its transformation into a thousand-mile-wide extra-tropical monster and its unexpected left turn, pushing the Atlantic Ocean smack onto Long Beach Island.

In *Surviving Sandy*, the author explains the unique weather systems that made Superstorm Sandy such a deadly storm. He also brings the storm to life as readers experience Sandy through the recollections of Islanders who stayed, many to their regret.

In Holgate, "Fire company safety officer Stanley Markowski III could not believe he was looking at Holgate. He saw cars on top of buildings, buildings flipped over on top of themselves, houses inside of houses, houses gone..."

In Beach Haven, Charlie Potter and Willy Logue, two employees of the Sea Shell Resort motel, heard a "thunderous crack" when a massive wave smashed through the boarded-up window, pushed the heavy beer cooler toward the men and pinned them against the bar.

In Ship Bottom, thirty inches of water poured into the borough hall in eight minutes. The waves on flooded bayside streets knocked Patrolman Brian Tretola off the small boat he was using to rescue residents from homes inundated by the bay. The water was so deep that he went in over his head.

Surf City resident Andy Warren experienced both ends of Sandy. When it was a hurricane in the Caribbean his cruise was diverted to avoid the storm. Back home, he saw his sister-in-law knocked over by strong waves on the Boulevard in North Beach. He said, "I've never seen anything like it in my life."

In Harvey Cedars, Superintendent of Public Works Lloyd Vosseller prepared for the worse but hoped for the best. And the best is what Harvey Cedars got. Protected by a two-year-old beach replenishment project, the town that lost almost half of its homes in 1962 sustained only limited damage this time.

Long Beach Island has a history of hurricanes and northeasters barreling over our dunes, the ocean meeting the bay. The 1821 storm was the only hurricane in recorded history, until Sandy, in which the eye came ashore in New Jersey. It destroyed the cedar forests here and greatly narrowed our barrier island. In the 1889 hurricane, Beach Haven Terrace was "an open sea covered with white caps." A northeaster in 1935 destroyed the railroad bridge to the Island; cut the Beach Haven fishing pier in half; took out Harvey Cedars' protective sea wall and pushed two feet of water into downtown Beach Haven. The 1944 hurricane, the worst storm since before the Civil War, destroyed twenty percent of Harvey Cedars' homes and washed Holgate's few homes into the bay.

Then the three-day northeaster in March 1962, in which five high tides cut the Island in thirds, destroyed all the dunes, damaged most of the oceanfront homes and deposited a Navy destroyer on the beach in Holgate, which again lost most of its homes and businesses to the rage of the Atlantic Ocean.

And then came Superstorm Sandy, a combination of hurricane and northeaster, with its hell, havoc and destructive rage. This is its story.

Margaret Thomas Buchholz
Co-Author, *Great Storms of the Jersey Shore*

Introduction

We love storms. They excite us and frighten us, exhilarate us and awe us, intrigue us and entertain us. They can heal us — negative ions from lightning storms have a tranquilizing effect — inspire us — from tales of Zeus hurling thunderbolts on Mount Olympus to Rip van Winkle bowling with dwarfs in the Catskills — refresh us — rain is water that has been distilled by the sun — and humble us — Mother Nature still rules.

At the same time we curse the winds that blow down our homes and the flash floods that wash them away, as well as sudden showers that spoil picnics and sleet that turns streets into skating rinks.

We get all sorts of storms on the Jersey coast — thunderstorms, snowstorms, squalls, gales, hurricanes, cyclones, monsoons, a tornado now and then, 100-year storms, 500-year storms, even "perfect" storms. Living at the edge of a large land mass on the shore of a major body of water, we've become as familiar with storm varieties as Eskimos are with types of snow.

Now we can add "superstorm" to that list.

But... what is a superstorm?

It's easy enough to ID a northeaster and a southwester; they're regular visitors in these parts. It's a bit tougher to know the difference between a squall and a gale unless you've spent some time at sea. Hurricanes come in a distinctive shape that's immediately recognizable, but they are the trickiest to track, rolling over the open sea feeding on the warm summer waters, sometimes plowing ahead like a bull, other times turning and twisting like a ballet dancer.

Thanks to satellites we can watch them being born as tropical disturbances off the coast of Africa, then moving westward across the Atlantic, growing in strength and size into tropical storms, perhaps becoming hurricanes lurching across the Caribbean and into the Gulf, heading for Texas or Louisiana, or hitting Bermuda and suddenly turning north toward Cape Hatteras and Cape May. We watch each one like a sports event: Will it go out to sea or hit land, and where and how hard? Forecasters keep an eye on their computers the way gamblers watch the roulette wheel. They track its possible deaths — alone and un-mourned at sea or in a final gasp of destruction on land.

The storm that came ashore here on October 29, 2012, had been in our sights from the beginning. It was a bit late in the hurricane season, which runs from June through November. Most of the big blows come in August and September. There have been years where the schedule is off a bit; it takes time to warm up an ocean. It was catalogued, named, measured and rated as it grew from tropical storm to hurricane, then back again, then up again and down again until all bets were off.

So, what was it? It wasn't a "storm of the century" as some began to call it; the century was far too young to entertain nominations for that title; with 87 seasons to go and a climate in the midst of change, other contenders could be expected. By the time it roared into the Jersey coast it had been officially downgraded to tropical storm status; that seemed dreadfully inadequate in light of the havoc it wreaked. But by any measure it was one of the fiercest and costliest storms in our recorded history.

So we called it "Superstorm Sandy."

Our homegrown blows are northeasters. They can be nasty, too, and unpredictable but they don't need warm water. In fact one of the biggest and most destructive arrived in a snowstorm in March 1962, and stayed through five high tides, flooding the shore, shattering boardwalks and oceanfront homes, lifting bayside homes off their blocks to float about like bumper cars, and pushing whole dunes onto the roads.

That storm was generally considered to be more destructive than any hurricane in these parts had ever been. It prompted communities all along the shore to revise their building codes, warning systems and emergency management procedures.

Northeasters weren't given names, but the weather gurus felt a storm that intense deserved something more memorable than "that big blow we had in '62." For a while it was referred to as the "Ash Wednesday Storm" for the day it showed up, but the U.S. Weather Service soon dubbed it "The Great Atlantic Storm," the only northeaster ever to get an official name. Until Sandy came along the Great Atlantic Storm — known as the '62 Storm — was generally considered the greatest storm to hit the Jersey shore.

We like to measure things, rate them, compare them, and the arguments have begun between the '62 Storm and Superstorm Sandy. How do we measure — wind speed, rainfall, size, duration, beaches washed away, homes destroyed?

In the comprehensive history *Great Storms of the Jersey Shore*, all the great storms were described, ranked and compared, and the debate began over which was the greatest. It came down to the fall hurricane of 1944, which tore up boardwalks and toppled beachfront homes, or the 1962 northeaster, which covered the streets with sand and lifted houses off their lots and floated them away to sea.

Hurricanes pack a much stronger punch than northeasters — starting at 75 mph for Category 1 and up — while northeasters get about half that. But hurricanes move much faster than their lumbering cousins; if it comes ashore in the morning, it's usually gone by evening.

The '62 Storm parked itself over the Jersey shore for three days, blowing and pounding. The storm pushed through the inlets, filling the back bays where the spring tides kept it bottled up

But storms aren't measured by wind and water alone. Destruction has a dollar figure. And here comparisons are pointless. In 50 years, land values and building costs have ballooned, as well as taxes and insurance. In addition, programs for safety and emergency management need more funding.

The Jersey shore has endured and largely survived all the storms that have come its way. There have been losses, such as Tuckers Island, which stood just off the southern end of Long Beach Island, a community of homes and a lighthouse which succumbed to a storm in 1927. Long Beach Island itself has lost acreage to storms over the years, with some cutting the Island into several short beach islands.

"We're stronger than the storm," we said after Superstorm Sandy.

We may not be stronger than the great storms to come. But we are smarter. If the ice caps continue to melt, the sea level continues to rise, the beaches are not regularly reinforced, development not regulated, then people a hundred years from now might say, "We should have listened to Sandy.

LARRY SAVADOVE
CO-AUTHOR, *GREAT STORMS OF THE JERSEY SHORE*

Preface

It just *happened*. No warning. No notice. The serenity acquired through almost twenty years of rebuilding and new development lost in a savage series of storm-driven high tide cycles. The new moon — hiding behind a churning vortex of clouds, rain and snow — worked its deadly magic, driving spring tides even higher. Wind, snow and waves thrashed, ripped, shredded. No way around it: This was the end.

The dunes struggled to contain the ferocity of the ocean during those three days in March of 1962 as the northeaster gorged itself on life and property along the Jersey Shore. But dunes are made of sand, tiny grains of crushed rock and shell. They stood no chance at all. Neither did roads and structures standing unguarded and ever more vulnerable with each successive high tide. Eventually, parts of Long Beach Island became part of the Atlantic. And the cycle continued through time and tide, and the Island became even more unrecognizable.

For Island inhabitants, each tide cycle brought a worse nightmare. Homes got pushed from foundations and piling. Some moved. Some shifted. Some were relegated to scrap wood. Some vanished entirely into the murky, cold water — gone without a trace. In Harvey Cedars, a new inlet formed. All over the Island, roads and sidewalks disappeared under feet of sand. On the southern end, in Holgate, Bond's Coast Guard station would be called back into duty as a lifesaving station as desperate refugees sought shelter. Some wouldn't make it.

Everything was backwards after that 1962 northeaster, formally named The Great Atlantic Storm by the U.S. Weather Bureau but forever known by local residents as the '62 Storm. Nothing seemed the way it was. Much of the work residents put into rebuilding, restructuring and developing Long Beach Island after the 1944 hurricane was washed away. And less than two decades after the Atlantic City Hurricane, another generation watched the end of another chapter of Island history.

But it was also the beginning of a new one.

The '62 Storm might have erased what was, but it didn't get it all. The sand in the Boulevard had barely dried when officials began the long process of recovery and rebuilding. The damage was extensive, especially in Harvey Cedars and Holgate. The storm had affected everyone who called the Island home, and life was decidedly different. But in essence, it also represented a violent birth, the beginning of a new chapter that would see the Island grow into one of the most popular and economically successful resorts on the Jersey Shore.

From the tumult of sea-foam-laden chaos emerged five decades of intense development. Two generations of residents and visitors would enjoy Long Beach Island, building incredible memories along the way. Each successive summer season brought more cars, larger homes, and new forms of entertainment, dining and shopping outlets.

By the end of the 1960s, Long Beach Island was not just alive, it was kicking with new life. It wasn't instant, of course. Years of hard work went into getting the Island going. But once it hit its stride, the growth didn't stop. Those fifty years of growth are filled with the memories and experiences of several generations. Some of us recall hanging out at the Disco at Silver Sands Marina in Holgate and riding go-karts at Hartman's. We visited the schooner *Lucy Evelyn*, and watched Bay Village emerge from a group of tiny bayside shacks. We enjoyed an evening program at the Foundation of Arts and Sciences or at the Long Beach Island Historical Museum. Took sunset cruises on the Black Whale. Traded in our tokens at Mr. Tee's. Saw Bruce Springsteen at Le Garage. Rented a surrey as a kid and pretended to drive for the first time.

We all have our memories of our Long Beach Island. Our block. Our dunes. Our beach. We recall precisely the way the sun falls on the sand and how the shadows dance as the dune grass sways in the sea breeze. We know where to find the best coffee and the nicest lifeguard. We remember our favorite place to putt, our favorite beach to ride the waves, our favorite place to grab a bite or have a beer. We know the best place to watch a sunset or a summer storm — or to just be enveloped by the deep blues and purples of the approaching night as it chases the pinks, yellows and brilliant oranges beyond the western horizon.

We all have our own Long Beach Island experiences, but we share many as well. One of the most antiquated yet unifying experiences of so many has been the drive-by pilgrimage to the Shack. The "little shack that could" stood valiantly year after year after year. From paintings and postcards to family photo albums and even its own documentary, the little shack was a visual representation of the heart of Long Beach Island. It was our first welcome to the other world we all enjoyed, away from that real world we left to the west. The Shack would weather and wear as years went by, but it stayed up to greet each new season with a nostalgic and comforting hello that no other manmade structure could quite match.

Those feelings and experiences had lasted long into the twilight of yet another summer season as the last of the visitors and summer residents headed home in late October of 2012. For many, it would be the last they would see of their era of Long Beach Island.

High above, the moon was nearing its full phase, and a trio of weather systems was taking position. Within days, those systems would begin their atmospheric, hydraulic and cosmic game of chess. And for much that was in their way, the end was coming once more.

SCOTT MAZZELLA

1962: Harvey Cedars. This aerial view of the High Point section shows where the legendary northeaster cut a new inlet from ocean to bay at 79th Street.

NOAA's GOES-13 satellite captured this visible image of the massive Hurricane Sandy on October 28 at 9:02 a.m. EDT. The line of clouds from the Gulf of Mexico north are associated with the cold front that Sandy is merging with. Sandy's western cloud edge is already over the mid-Atlantic and northeastern United States.

LATE OCTOBER, 2012:

The Approaching Storm

CHAPTER ONE

Goodbye Blue Sky

Jim Mahoney did not like what he was seeing. It was the last week of October 2012 and his job as a resident field service engineer for ABB had him stuck in a small town outside of York, Pa., as the weather forecasts for a hurricane named Sandy kept getting worse. He knew weather and he knew what his gut was telling him. It wasn't going to be pretty.

Mahoney owns a home in Holgate, and if walls could talk, his walls would talk about Island storms until the seaweed harvesters come home. The Mahoney home is quaint — a touch of sea-breeze rustic with coral siding, beach trinkets festooning the property and the weathered-brass trademark "M" cemented into the front stoop. It's a house with storm roots that run deep.

The story Mahoney tells is that the house that had been on the lot was washed away in the hurricane of 1944, but the owner at the time bought a house that had been floating in the bay for $25 and moved it onto the property. Rooms have been added since, but it's the same house in the middle. Mahoney's father bought it in March 1959 and it has been in his family since.

Mahoney is one of the stalwart residents of Holgate, a tried-and-true man of the Island from the days it said "Bonds" on the water tower. After the '62 Storm, a very young Jim Mahoney watched his father put the house back on a higher foundation after three days of disastrous high tides washed it — and just about every other nearby house — off its footings. The family never sunk a lot of money into the house, figuring storms would always come along and do damage. Such realism is part of Mahoney's genuine beach blood.

But now, sitting in a power plant control room on a Saturday afternoon, all he could think of was getting back to Holgate to do what he could to protect his property. He wanted to cram his car with as many family treasures as it could hold and leave the Island. But at work, every passing minute felt like an hour. Eventually he put his foot down and told his boss he was leaving. It was 3 p.m. The desperation on his face must have been clear. His boss let him go.

Mahoney hit the road immediately, arriving on Long Beach Island at about 7 p.m. He spent the evening packing his car. Deciding what deserved a spot in what little room he had in his car was easy. He did all this the year before when Hurricane Irene rolled into town. He made sure his late parents' stuff got in alongside a few vintage Island maps, a photograph of the Silver Sands Marina and a number of other irreplaceable items. He even remembered how he had packed the car, so everything fit just right. A look at his watch revealed only two hours had passed.

Vinny, his neighbor across the street, was having a weekend gathering with the guys, so after the car was packed he went over to hang out, have a few drinks and trade stories. After a couple hours, as the hands on the clock ticked past midnight, the guys took their beers to the beach. Walking past the Jacqueline Avenue post and up the old wooden beach ramp like they have countless times before, the men toasted the storm as a stiff wind whistled in the dune grass around them.

"This could be the last one of these!" Vinny said as they stared out towards the sea. Mahoney wasn't sure if Vinny was talking about the storm or the weekend parties without the wives. He was afraid to ask.

On Sunday Mahoney wandered about, taking pictures, looking at the neighborhood, walking on the beach, hoping it would all be the same in a couple days. The wind had picked up, the ocean was pretty choppy and waves were already lapping the dunes. He gave his house a last long look, locked the doors, got in the car and slowly drove up the Island to the Causeway. Storm preparations were taking place everywhere — people boarding windows, putting sandbags in doorways. He stopped by Brant Beach to see how its recently replenished beaches were doing, thinking this would likely be a good test for them. The ocean had already devoured much of the new sand. Then he crossed the bridge and headed west to the suburbs of Philadelphia where he'd be staying for the next few days.

Mahoney was fortunate to get out when he did. That evening the relentless deluge of water entering the bay flooded roads around the Causeway and along the bayfront. As Mahoney's car crossed the Benjamin Franklin Bridge into Pennsylvania, Sandy was still far out in the Atlantic. But its path was becoming clearer. For the next 24 hours the world would watch Sandy take aim at the beaches of the Garden State.

Bayshore Drive, Barnegat

CHAPTER TWO

Let the Wind Blow

The story of Sandy actually began a couple of weeks earlier as a freight train of trade winds blowing in from the east pushed a wave of super hot air above the arid sands of the Sahara desert.

As that wave approached the Sudan region, the harsh desert changed into a less arid savanna. There, the hot, dry air mixed with the warm, moist air from the forests below. When the different types of air met, they clashed. The air condensed and cooled, and clouds, rain and eventually thunderstorms formed.

This cluster of storms moved off the coast of Senegal, Africa, on October 11, 2012, riding a ripple in the jet stream west. The tropical wave floundered as it met resistance from several weather systems heading west across the Intertropical Convergence Zone, an area along the equator that wraps the Earth in a belt of clouds and thunderstorm activity. Water evaporating from the ocean sent more warm, moist air into the atmosphere, where it condensed and formed more clouds and rain. That process of changing the warm water vapor into clouds and rain creates latent heat. As more heat was created, more instability occurred. The clouds grew taller and wider as the evaporating ocean water spiraled up a column of air at the center of the storm's circulation. As the clouds grew, more rain formed. Thunderstorms grew. The process kept the tropical wave moving.

The wave entered the eastern Caribbean on October 18 with barely a whimper. The only real evidence of life coming in the form of a shift in light winds over the Windward Islands. Ever so slowly and efficiently, thunderstorms gravitated toward the center of low pressure developing within the wave.

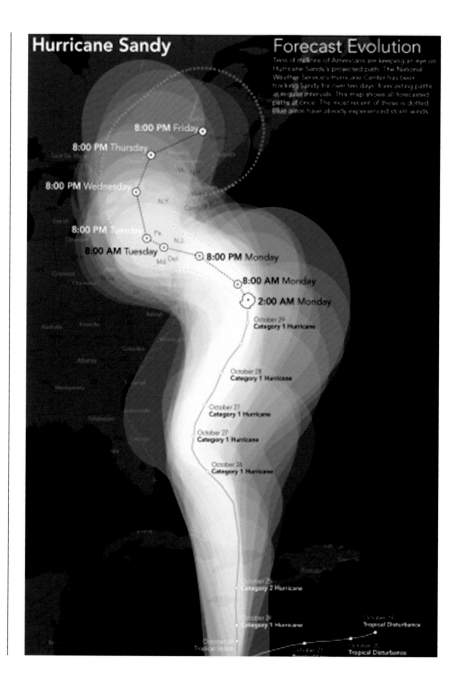

Suomi NPP - VIIRS Day Night Band - Oct. 29 2012 (Night)

M S S

As Hurricane Sandy made landfall on the New Jersey coast during the night of October 29, a NASA/NOAA polar-orbiting satellite captured this infrared view of the storm. This image by University of Wisconsin-Madison is a composite of several satellite passes over North America taken 16 to18 hours before Sandy's landfall. The graphic on the facing page shows the evolution of Hurricane Sandy forecasts.

By Saturday, October 20, rain began to fall in somewhat organized bands. Meteorologists at the National Hurricane Center took note and the tropical wave earned a new name, 99L. On Sunday, high pressure over the Gulf of Mexico and the southwest Atlantic strengthened the low-pressure system. Warm water temperatures provided an ample source of energy. As 99L moved about 200 miles south of Jamaica, more thunderstorms developed around the center. The storm's circulation became visible in satellite images, the National Hurricane Center updated forecasts to show a system in the Caribbean that could develop into something significant.

By Monday, October 22, it had. Overnight, NASA's Tropical Rainfall Measuring Mission satellite watched 99L's precipitation closely. Its data was telling. Deep convection had formed near the center. Among the thunderstorms surrounding the center was one with "hot towering." That meant some of the storms reached heights of over nine miles. Those storms released a tremendous amount of latent heat, which acted as a supercharger for the storm. As its center churned roughly 305 nautical miles south-southwest of Kingston, Jamaica, it reached its next significant milestone. The National Hurricane Center upgraded 99L to Tropical Depression 18, the eighteenth tropical wave in the Atlantic to become this strong during the 2012 hurricane season. An alarmingly rapid intensification followed and the TD18 designation lasted only hours. At 11 a.m., the National Hurricane Center issued a tropical storm watch for Jamaica. Reconnaissance data showed winds sustained at 39 mph by 2 p.m. Tropical systems earn a name when they reach this milestone, and this tropical storm was named Sandy.

Day and night, computer models in the United States, Canada and Europe took in data. As early as Saturday, October 21, the Canadian model, the Global Forecast System and the European Center for Medium Range Weather Forecasts, commonly known as the Euro model, all showed the system affecting the East Coast of the United States at some point in the next week to 10 days. The models indicated a hybrid storm with a hurricane steering close enough to the East Coast to merge with a trough of low pressure digging in near the Ohio River Valley. This merging of a powerful trough and a hurricane is an unusual phenomenon. When it happens, it can create a storm of fantastic proportion. It becomes a

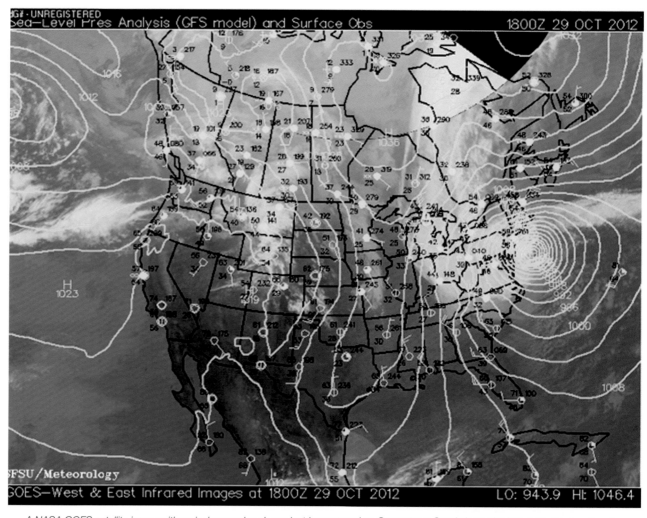

A NASA GOES satellite image with an isobar overlay shows just how wound up Superstorm Sandy is as she heads for the coast on the afternoon of October 29. At this point the storm is extratropical and the windfield is many times that of a typical hurricane.

storm conceived with the warm core of a hurricane that explodes into a cold-cored beast many times the size of a typical hurricane.

The last time the Atlantic basin experienced such a storm was 1991. The famous Halloween Storm of that autumn combined a powerful northeaster

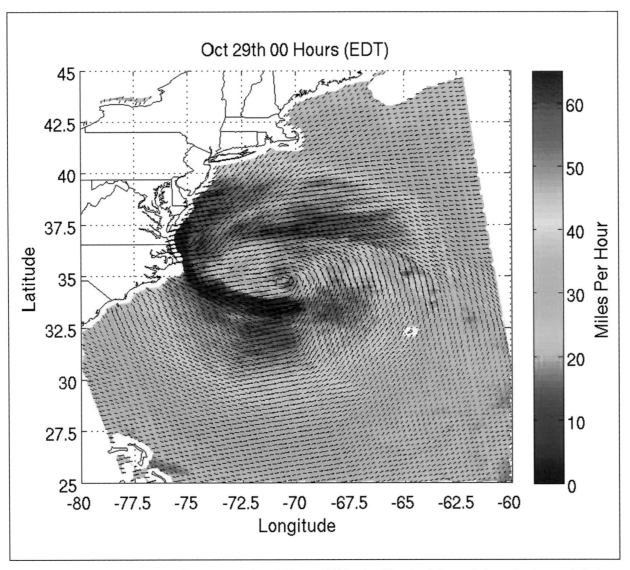

Oct 29th 00 Hours (EDT)

Ocean surface winds for Hurricane Sandy observed at 12:00 a.m. EDT October 29; colors indicate wind speed and arrows indicate direction. The image shows the large extent of high winds associated with this system, and uses radar scatterometry which enables frequent, more than once per day, observations of Earth's winds over the ocean.

and a weakening Hurricane Grace. The hybrid system brought damaging waves and flooding to the East Coast, including the Jersey Shore. Waves up to 30 feet pounded the coast, particularly in Massachusetts, leaving many shore homes severely damaged. The storm gained fame in Sebastian Junger's book *The Perfect Storm* and subsequent movie of the same name, which told the harrowing story of the sinking of the fishing vessel *Andrea Gail.*

That storm was on the minds of meteorologists, storm fanatics, surfers and others with an awareness and understanding of weather as they watched the models on October 21. The Perfect Storm of 1991 unleashed most of its fury on the open sea. Realizing the impact a storm like that could have over land, many meteorologists began discussing predictions in weather blogs. Before long, hints of what was looming hit social media.

Mark Sudduth, of HurricaneTrack. com, one of the more widely known hurricane tracking groups, was the first to discuss the predictions to the broader public. The banner headline for his blog on October 22 read, "A storm for the ages? Perhaps. First, it is a Caribbean concern." Sandy was barely on anyone's radar along the East Coast, but Sudduth was already reading tea leaves and seeing serious trouble brewing.

"There are very few instances when I have posted a headline like the one in this blog," Sudduth posted on October 22. "Hype is not a tool I use to get the attention of my audience unless it is warranted and I feel that it could help save lives and property. What I am seeing in some of the global models is worthy of getting your attention and if it's hype, then all the better in the long run."

While the Global Forecast System model began to favor a path that had Sandy, or what was left of Sandy, heading far out into the Atlantic, the Euro model continued showing something remarkable: A mid-900 millibar low situated right off the mid-Atlantic coastline — the isobars, lines of equal barometric pressure, packed incredibly tight, pressure gradients so great the wind damage would be devastating hundreds of miles from the center. On October 22 AccuWeather meteorologist Elliot Abrams commented about it in his daily blog. "A storm like the one depicted would be disastrous in the Middle Atlantic states, threatening death and serious injury and causing billions of dollars in damage. If this were to actually happen and hurricane-force winds hit places like Philadelphia and New York City, there would be a major storm surge, massive power outages, flooding rain..."

At this point, the big question was whether or not the models would change, something forecasting models are known to do frequently. A disaster in the making on one model might show up as a brief rain shower in Duck, North Carolina, in the next. With such uncertainty, forecasters called for caution and awareness, but fell back on the idea that everyone needed to wait to see what the models would do in coming days. In the meantime, Tropical Storm Sandy was about to make a move. The most immediate threat came to those living in the Caribbean. Sandy had set its sights on Jamaica.

It had been twenty-four years since Jamaica experienced a direct hit from a hurricane, but at 8 a.m. on October 24, aircraft reconnaissance data showed Sandy at hurricane strength and Jamaica sitting directly in its path. Only eighty nautical miles south of Kingston, Hurricane Sandy advanced toward shore. The National Hurricane Center issued a tropical storm warning for the central Bahamas and posted tropical storm watches in parts of southeastern Florida.

On Wednesday, October 24, at 3 p.m., Hurricane Sandy slammed into Bull Bay, Jamaica, as a Category 1 storm with winds of 86 mph. Haiti, located to the east of Jamaica and within the northeast quadrant of the

As the storm approached, all eyes were on the surf at beach entrances (above), and on forecasts on smart phones (facing page).

	am	pm
Verizon	**9:30**	**9%**
	Long Beach Island, NJ	
	48° NE 6 mph	62°	2.3 ft 6 s	L- 12:39 PM H- 6:26 AM
TODAY	1-3 ft	2-4 ft
SUNDAY	3-5 ft	5-7 ft
MONDAY	10-15 ft	12-16 ft
TUESDAY	6-10 ft	6-10 ft
WEDNESDAY	5-7 ft	4-6 ft
THURSDAY	2-4 ft	2-4 ft
FRIDAY	1-3 ft	2+ ft

Updated: 10/27/12, 9:29

Signs of the times: the m. t. burton gallery in Surf City battens down and leaves a message.

hurricane, experienced heavy rain and flooding on an epic scale. Fifty-four people were killed. Three more were killed and 24,500 homes damaged in the Dominican Republic. And Hurricane Sandy was just getting started. It emerged from the northern coast of Jamaica, immediately fed off the deep, warm waters of the Cayman Trench, and became a much more organized storm. Winds increased overnight. Next in the path sat Cuba, where shortly after 1 a.m. on Thursday, October 25, a Category 3 Hurricane

Sandy made a second landfall. Wind speeds reached 115 mph, with one 143 mph gust recorded. Eleven people were killed and 17,000 homes destroyed.

Meanwhile, southeast Florida began feeling some of the effects. Fort Lauderdale's Ocean Rescue ordered beachgoers out of the water. Winds had gusted above 40 mph, with 50 mph gusts reported at Crandon Park on Key Biscayne.

In the early morning of Saturday, October 27, Sandy moved north of the Bahamas and into the open Atlantic, underwent a brief weakening cycle and by 8 a.m. was downgraded to a tropical storm. As it weakened, it doubled in size, with tropical storm force winds extending 870 nautical miles from the center — twice as far as they had reached when Sandy hit Cuba. Sandy regained hurricane strength and became the largest tropical cyclone since such measurements started in 1988. The cloud canopy reached over 1,000 miles in diameter. Meteorologists at the National Hurricane Center also noticed other differences in structure. Hurricane Sandy was hinting that it was far from typical.

CHAPTER THREE

The Uncertainty of Being Certain

By Thursday, October 25, as Hurricane Sandy destroyed much of eastern Cuba, the possibility of it hitting the mid-Atlantic Coast became more likely. The Euro model showed a massive tropical system heading into the Delmarva Peninsula perpendicular to shore, leaving most of southern New Jersey in the most devastating quadrant of a hurricane — the northeast quadrant. There, high winds and a massive storm surge are possible. Other models, while still in agreement for the most part, showed variations. Some showed a direct hit to New England, others a path to the Canadian Maritimes.

The national media ramped up coverage. The big question: Would an Irene-weary public buy into the idea of another massive storm knocking at their front door?

The New Jersey Office of Emergency Management, the Governor's Office and the National Weather Service in Mount Holly had already begun planning. At the same time, all of the mayors on Long Beach Island and in Stafford, Barnegat, and Tuckerton were watching. Storm forecasts like this did not come along often. The leaders in these towns were not comforted by the near miss of Hurricane Irene. They considered Hurricane Irene a bullet dodged.

There are tales of people, sometimes Native Americans, sometimes kids, depending on the story, who put their ears to railroad tracks to tell if a train is coming. As the stories go, the rails vibrate ever so slightly and sensitive eardrums pick up the sound. The indication that a train is coming is determined long before you see or actually hear it. In this case, if Hurricane Sandy were the train, surfers were the fortunetellers. They didn't have ears to a steel rail, but rather bodies immersed in a warm autumn ocean, eyes scanning the horizon for

Emergency preparations include pet carriers (above) at the High Point Volunteer Fire Co. At right, the ocean chews away at dunes in Harvey Cedars.

incoming swells. If any group fuses mind, body and soul with the ocean, winds and weather, it is the community of dedicated surfers who tame the waves that arrive on our shores.

Surfers know the effects of weather and wind on the ocean. Their goal is to find out as much as possible about the weather so they are ready for good surf when it happens. They constantly listen to the tracks. But surfers are not an entity unto themselves. They are members of the larger community. They work in the stores and wait the tables. They are landscapers, builders, students, journalists and teachers. They are also firefighters and police officers. When the surfing community senses something epic, word gets out. This is how emergency management sometimes works at the shore.

The surfers knew about Sandy about eight days prior to landfall. They did not know if, when or where Sandy would hit, but they were watching. Their anticipation found its way to police stations and firehouses, where talk

of the approaching storm began. This makes all the difference when it comes to preparedness. The fact that emergency responders were considering the possibility of such a storm had authorities thinking about those "what if" questions. A week out, Island residents were abuzz about Sandy.

The hope was that it would be a typical hurricane, the kind that growls at the shore as it swings by a hundred miles east of the Island, the kind that brings sunny skies and epic big surf. But as the days went by, Sandy looked less and less like a surfing event. By Friday, October 26, it looked more like a storm that could destroy the shore.

Meanwhile, conversations intensified between the mayors of Long Beach Island's five municipalities. They held regular meetings. Throughout the week, the mayors of Stafford, Tuckerton and Barnegat joined in. If the worst were to happen, each town would be affected by the needs of the others. Long Beach Township is divided by the other Island municipalities and would have to coordinate with other towns throughout evacuation processes. Every person on the Island must pass through the gateway created by the Route 72 causeway bridges. That is Stafford's territory, so the municipalities would need to work together to run any evacuation operations.

By Friday, all eyes were on the forecasts. The models refined their predictions and the focus shifted south toward the Delmarva Peninsula. That put the eye of Sandy just south of Long Beach Island, a worst-case scenario as it puts southern Ocean County in the northeast quadrant of the storm, the area with the highest winds, most rain and worst storm surge. If Sandy were to transform into a cold-core, extratropical system, the situation would be similar, although the rain and wind threat would be more widespread and the surge would come in over a much wider area.

New Jersey Governor Chris Christie had been campaigning in North Carolina for Republican presidential candidate Mitt Romney. On Friday, he canceled the remainder of his agenda in North Carolina as well as a scheduled trip to Nevada the following week.

Upon arriving back in New Jersey, Christie began official state disaster preparations. He directed his cabinet to mobilize statewide response networks. At 8 p.m. Friday, the State Emergency Operations Center was activated and staffing began immediately. New Jersey's Regional Operations and Intelligence Center and the state Offices of Emergency Management continued to monitor Hurricane Sandy as it spiraled in the Atlantic as a Category 2 storm. All county offices of emergency management were contacted, and emergency plans were

initiated at the state, county and local level.

On Long Beach Island and the surrounding Mainland communities, mayors continued to meet and conference calls with the state began. The situation was similar to a year earlier, when most of the same plans and operations were put in place for Hurricane Irene. But Sandy was a different animal, and local government was aware of the possibilities.

On Friday, the mayors met in Harvey Cedars and discussed topics ranging from how to deal with the "Irene Effect" to evacuation timing. The National Weather Service was included on a conference call and it reported a more severe situation for the Jersey Shore. The mayors decided not to wait for the state. They called for voluntary evacuations of the entire island immediately, with thoughts of building up to a mandatory evacuation no later than Sunday afternoon. They feared residents were not taking Sandy seriously.

Towns moved their fire trucks, ambulances and heavy equipment to Stafford, keeping only equipment necessary for rescue and law enforcement. Ship Bottom Police Chief Paul Sharkey contacted the National Guard, requesting trucks and personnel that can handle significant flooding. The National Guard provided a Humvee and a military-grade, 2½ ton "deuce," which can operate in water up to thirty inches deep.

Houses in northwestern Monmouth County vibrated slightly as the thunderous roar of two army green National Guard Blackhawk helicopters escorting Governor Christie's New Jersey State Police AgustaWestland AW139

Storm tides that crossed the dunes of Long Beach Island (facing page) filled the bay and then the streets on the Mainland as well (above), on Bayshore Drive in Barnegat.

Sandy Hook to Cape May as of Sunday, October 28, at 4 p.m. He ordered Atlantic City to evacuate the casinos as well.

Back on Long Beach Island, police and fire crews took the governor's message to the streets. Firefighters and police officers slowly cruised every block alerting the residents they needed to evacuate. The message boomed through loudspeakers, echoing eerily through the mostly empty streets.

For a storm predicted so far out in advance, residents spent the week of October 22 talking about Sandy, but it seemed as though many were expecting news that Hurricane Sandy's track had changed. They figured Sandy would veer off into the Atlantic, as is usually the case with tropical systems north of Cape Hatteras. Chatter was more "Think it will happen?" than "I better get to my shore house and board it up!" Thus, Long Beach Island's houses, especially those that were not primary residences, looked ready

pierced the Saturday morning air on October 27. The helicopters landed in East Keansburg for a governor's briefing. Overnight, the forecasts left no doubt. Sandy was going to hit New Jersey. It mattered little if she slammed into Sandy Hook or Cape May. One way or another, New Jersey was getting hit.

Governor Christie was no longer in campaign mode. He was in his "Get the hell off the beach" mode — a phrase he won praise for during New Jersey's preparations for Hurricane Irene. Christie announced a state of emergency for the entire state, and ordered mandatory evacuations of the barrier islands from

for a beach weekend and not for a hurricane. There were plenty of boarded-up businesses, but the number of boarded-up homes, or even homes with minimal preparations, was hardly noticeable.

Off the coast of New Jersey, wave heights were already approaching 20 feet. No one had ever seen a hurricane with a cloud canopy so large, more than 1,000 miles in diameter. Tropical storm force winds extended for hundreds of miles. And to make matters worse, Hurricane Sandy showed signs of developing a new eye. Sandy was strengthening.

CHAPTER FOUR

Final Approach

Along the Jersey Shore, Hurricane Sandy pumped wind-driven swells onto the beaches, and through the inlets. Back bays swelled for almost two days prior to the storm. Water flowed in the inlets with each high tide, but the winds kept it from flowing out when the tide ebbed. From Saturday night through the height of the storm, water just kept coming in.

There is only so much room in the bay. The water steadily advanced through Little Egg Inlet on one end of the Island and Barnegat Inlet on the other. Northeast winds drove more water south from Barnegat Bay. It poured into Little Egg Harbor from underneath the Causeway bridges and was held there by the wind. As the last of the evacuees made it over the bridges at 4 p.m. on Sunday, the bay level was rising steadily.

When the bridges shut down for public use, almost 2,000 people remained on Long Beach Island. Like many along the coast, Doug Raylman tried to figure out just how the storm would play out. Was the media bark genuine? Were the residents taking it seriously? The pulse of the crowd at the local Super Fresh in Manahawkin where Raylman was shopping provided little evidence either way. "The store didn't seem too crazy yesterday," he told a reporter for *The SandPaper.* "I was prepared for a madhouse, but it didn't really seem like people were getting that upset. There's a lot of hype, and the media is saying this is a totally different storm than Irene. I think they're trying to make sure people are prepared because they kind of dropped the ball on that the last time."

Residents placed items in their homes as high as they could. And they stocked up on necessities — non-perishable food and water. But overall, the feeling of those who stayed was that Sandy might be rough, but not a storm they couldn't ride out.

While some of those who stayed on Long Beach Island grew concerned about their decision, others had no such qualms. Blogger and *SandPaper*

There was nowhere for the rising tide to go but up, over streets, into homes and buildings, all the way into the woods on the mainland. At left, the edge of the Cedar Run marshlands. Above, the view at the High Point Volunteer Fire Co., Harvey Cedars.

managing editor Jay Mann was one. He stayed and chronicled much of the storm through posts and his video camera. He also served as a reporter and official observer for the National Weather Service, and his observations and insights splashed into the public realm in social media updates. For many of those off the Island who worried about their homes, Mann's updates — "Jay Mann Chronicles the Storm" — provided an essential source of information:

Sunday, October 28, 2012:

I guess this is the relative calm before the storm. With the bewitching evacuation hour (4 p.m.) now past, the roads are quiet, though not eerily so.

The toughest go has been trying to find java or colder energy drinks.

I ran into a couple guys who had to cruise all the way up to the Ship Bottom 7-11 for even the minorist incidentals. And they just made it.

Talking with the 7-11 owners, they're afraid to stay open much longer (4:30) because

they were told by the police that folks will NOT be allowed to even leave the Island after 4.

That struck me as a tad cruel so I called LBTPD and was told that's potentially true. Any time after 4 pm, the police can deem it too unsafe to try to cross the Causeway bridges heading west.

I'm thinking — but dare not say it out loud — the last thing PDs want is to force people to stay ON the frickin' Island! Still, the option to do so falls under the extended powers given authorities under emergency circumstances. If winds kick it up to 70 mph, it's a no-go for zipping off the Island.

I even checked on the advisability of keeping the 7-11 open as a public service for emergency personnel but was told by the PD that coffee-ing and feeding of all must-stay folks has already been taken care of. Hmmm.

By the by, many/most ambulances have actually gone off-Island as a precautionary measure. It will, indeed be tough to hail an ambulance. Here's an excerpt from an FB thread: " ... first responders will NOT respond, at least from Ship Bottom south. Our orders are that we will respond IF POSSIBLE, only to Emergency Personnel. Aside from that all of our ambulances will be taken to the mainland. We will have only one 4WD response vehicle in each division. We are a very dedicated group, but it is a MANDATORY evacuation! Why should we risk our lives for people that think it brave, or romantic, or whatever to stay here. Believe me, if I had a choice I would be GONE. That is the truth about what will be happening, Jay."

Thanks for that info, Jim.

The first test of resolve — from stubborn stayers to emergency responders — came Sunday night when the first round of severe high tides crept into communities on both sides of the bay. It sent the bay over docks, bay beaches and bulkheads.

Sandy was still twenty-one hours away, but Long Beach Island was flooding. The usual spots got it the worst. Joey's Pizza in Beach Haven Crest, known for its flooding-induced "occasional waterfront dining" had flooded far above normal. In Beach Haven, photographs of popular attractions lit up social media — Borough Hall, the Chicken or the Egg and Fantasy Island in a sea of bay water, no roads or sidewalks in sight.

The first significant high tide showed clearly that Sandy was not Irene. Those who stayed on the Island, or in Tuckerton Beach, Mystic Islands, Cedar Bonnet Island, Beach Haven West, Mallard Island and low-lying areas of West Creek and Barnegat were about to see up-close what it takes to be a great storm on the Jersey Shore.

The 5th Street pavilion in Beach Haven is battered — and eventually taken — by the storm (left). Above, high surf approaches a beach entrance.

At this point, Hurricane Sandy was advancing north, but that would not last much longer. Two key elements determined where it would go next. First, an anomalous blocking pattern in the form of a system of high pressure set up just south of Greenland would prevent Sandy from continuing farther north. The air pattern around high-pressure systems moves clockwise and it coaxed Sandy in a western direction.

Helping this system out was a deep trough of low pressure that was digging through the Southeast. The trough pushed the jet stream deep into the south, reaching the northern fringes of the Gulf states. The jet stream then traveled up the eastern side of the trough, or right up the spine of the Appalachian Mountains and up and over the high pressure near Greenland. A deepening low-pressure system riding into that trough in the Midwest, its energy spinning counter-clockwise, eventually drew Hurricane Sandy in.

The final piece was simply a matter of timing. Not only was Sandy going to make landfall, it was going to do so during a full-moon-driven astronomical high tide.

On Monday, as authorities evacuated those on Long Beach Island who changed their minds, Sandy ventured into the cooler fall Atlantic Ocean water. Without the warm Gulf Stream, it started to weaken. But as it weakened, the energy bottled up in the center began spreading out as it unwound over the open Atlantic. That is what caused the winds to stretch so far. It was almost as though Hurricane Sandy took one last big exhale.

As Sandy transformed from tropical to extratropical, the regional National Weather Service offices and the National Hurricane Center debated what kinds of warnings should be posted. Sandy was not going to be a hurricane at landfall. Should hurricane warnings be posted, or should the National Weather Service use the warning systems utilized during northeasters? And how would that affect the public's perception of the storm?

Those questions inspired head meteorologist Gary Szatkowski to include a personal plea in a National Weather Service briefing that came out of Mount Holly, N.J. In the plea, which appeared on the last slide of a PowerPoint presentation, he begged people to err on the side of caution and provided

On Sunday, October 28th, some residents made a last-ditch effort to remove boats, but may have sacrificed their vehicles in the rising salt water (above, at Cedar Run Dock Road).

contact information for people to call him after the storm to criticize him if he was wrong. He even included a small image of some of the damage the '62 Storm did to the Jersey Shore. It was an unprecedented action from a top official at the National Weather Service.

The decision was made to stop using tropical watches and warnings and to go with regional office northeaster-type warning packages. The public would hear about Hurricane Sandy coming, but the wording they would see in warnings, forecasts and emergency management would no longer refer to a hurricane. It was a northeaster that packed the punch of a hurricane.

At 2 p.m. Monday afternoon, Sandy neared the end of its transformation into an extratropical system. Measurements taken by equipment dropped into the storm by hurricane-hunter aircraft showed that pressure had fallen to 940 millibars — the lowest ever recorded from a land-striking Atlantic storm north of Cape Hatteras, North Carolina. Sandy became fully extratropical by 5 p.m., only 45 nautical miles southeast of Atlantic City.

The structure of the storm was now completely different than a hurricane. Aside from the massive expansion, Sandy's core low-level temperatures were dropping. Most of the warmest air in the storm was now located in the northeast quadrant of its structure. Deep convection around the center was gone. Thunderstorms stopped around what had been the eye. Most of the rain in the storm moved to the southwest quadrant, an unusual development and completely contrary to a tropical system's characteristics.

This showed that Hurricane Sandy was a hurricane no more. But the threat Sandy posed had not lessened. In fact, Sandy was more dangerous than ever. A massive system would hit the Jersey Shore within hours. Sandy was something immense and powerful, and the public needed to know what it was up against. Some started throwing around a new term, one that even meteorologists would later admit was a name entirely fitting and appropriate. Sandy was now Superstorm Sandy.

As floodwaters rose, the only way out for residents who did not follow the mandatory evacuation orders was a ride in a truck like this, in Harvey Cedars (above).

CHAPTER FIVE

Leaving Home Ain't Easy

Judging by the number of fishermen staying at the Sea Shell Resort and Beach Club in Beach Haven, you would never guess a hurricane was coming. It was the weekend of the 16th Annual Striped Bass Fishing Derby. In an odd juxtaposition of fear and fishing, fishermen were bringing their boats onto the Island over the weekend while residents preparing for the hurricane were taking their boats off. The staff at the Shell had been kept busy all weekend, but by early Sunday afternoon people began to leave.

In the kitchen, Charlie Potter wrapped up his weekend shift. A year-round resident, Potter was also ending his season's work at the hotel and restaurant. Like most Islanders, he had an eye on the weather — and the clock. Hurricane or not, his job paid the bills, but he still had to get his family off the Island before the 4 p.m. evacuation deadline. No stranger to Island storms, he knew the flooding threat his home on Roosevelt Avenue in Holgate faced. They might even be without utilities. It was too risky for his girlfriend and their young son to stay, so Potter drove them to a relative's house in Barnegat to ride out the storm there.

Because of work, he had not prepared the house for the storm. He had to go back, which meant he would be riding out the storm in Holgate alone. He drove back before the causeway bridges closed and parked his truck at the Shell. He didn't want to lose his truck to flooding, and he figured it would be safer on the hotel's high ground between Engleside Avenue and Centre Street. He hitched a ride home from a coworker. He made non-perishable beef jerky and bottled up some fresh water in jugs.

In the back of his mind he thought Sandy's bark would be worse than her

bite. His family was safe on the Mainland, and if he got stuck on the Island he would have provisions to get him through. Still, he packed a bag just in case he needed to make a quick escape.

A few blocks away members of the Bowker family busily prepared their home and business. The Bowkers have owned and operated Bowker's South Beach Deli & Grill in Holgate since 2009. The family home sits above the deli, just north of the municipal parking lot at the southern end of Long Beach Boulevard. When Sandy was still heading north in the Atlantic, Eileen Bowker grappled with how to deal with the storm. Her husband, Brian, was in Bloomington, Ind., with both daughters. The youngest, Emily, plays field hockey for the Hoosiers and had a game that weekend. Tagging along was their oldest daughter, Kayle, a volunteer firefighter in Beach Haven. With Brian and the girls away, Eileen was staring at the possibility of facing hurricane conditions with her two teenage sons, Brian Boru and Seon, and their 160-pound French mastiff, Otis.

Eileen had consulted with friends and neighbors. One neighbor, Dave Allerie, thought they were crazy for even considering staying. But he told Bowker that she and the boys could stay in his house if they needed to move to a higher building. Bowker called a friend in Beach Haven to seek his advice.

Most residents followed the mandatory evacuation orders, as posted, above, in North Beach. (Left) ScoJo's in Surf City recycles a message left for Irene.

"Aw hell, you're down in Holgate? It's going to be hard down there." He told her. "Just don't listen to the voices in your head."

She took a collaborative approach and asked her sons if they should leave. The boys were concerned about their neighborhood and the idea that no one would be there. They felt it was up to them to watch over their neighbors's homes. "If we leave, God won't protect the Island while we're gone," Brian told his mother. "God will protect the people that are here." They decided to stay.

The Bowkers stuffed backpacks and put them into dry bags. They lashed kayaks to piling. A surfing family, Eileen and her sons prepared their wetsuits in case they had to leave the house. They charged laptops, cell phones and other electronics. When they were done, they received a call from Eileen's husband, Brian. He was back in New Jersey with Kayla, but they couldn't get on the Island. The Causeway bridges had been shut down, so they headed to Burlington instead. Eileen again considered leaving, but word had spread that the bay had already risen and it was unlikely they would be able to get off.

With survival and evacuation preparations done, Bowker baked. The boys worked on school assignments. On occasion, Brian and Seon ventured out into the neighborhood they swore to watch over. They watched the ocean swell, checked on some homes and generally scouted out the area. They would have less than 24 hours before everything they were looking at would change dramatically.

Meanwhile, up and down the Island and along the bayshore, towns prepared as best they could. Public works employees carried trashcans, benches and other items off the beaches. All eyes on Sunday night focused on the bays, which continued to fill with water with each successive high tide. With each hour, more residents decided to leave, but many of those who stayed simply hunkered down, not knowing if it would be another Irene or another '62 Storm showing up the next day.

With another glance at the slate-gray sky above, Jim Mahoney walked from his packed car and up the stairs to his new second-floor apartment, feeling separated by every one of the eighty or so miles between him and his vulnerable Holgate home. The clouds appeared layered

Surf City.

above the house in Upper Darby, Pa., a suburb just west of Philadelphia. The lower level clouds moved quickly from east to west. Sandy's outermost machinations were busy going about their work. Distracted by thoughts of Superstorm Sandy's potential, Jim's inner autopilot took care of mundane actions like unlocking the front door. He felt keyed in to the storm.

He opened the door. The apartment was sparsely furnished - with not even a television. It was only his second night in the apartment since he and his

wife Susan began renting it from her father. They had yet to move the usual trappings into the place. In fact, his car — now full of his Holgate treasures — held more of the comforts of home than this apartment. But he had what he needed to ride out the storm — an inflatable mattress, a laptop, a cell phone with internet capability and a crank-powered emergency radio he brought back from the Shore.

Mahoney connected his phone to his laptop to get information during the

Holgate.

storm. With a few keystrokes, he checked Sandy's strength and direction. The forecast was still putting southern New Jersey in the crosshairs. He got on the phone to call Susan, who was in South Carolina visiting her grandkids. Susan was hoping to drive back up to Rochester, N.Y., on Monday. "Don't come up during the storm," Mahoney pleaded with her. "You'll probably be fine on the inland roadways but once you get to Virginia you're going to hit trouble." Her plan was to stop by Upper Darby and then head on up to upstate New York, but Jim convinced her otherwise. She would wait.

Mahoney looked around. The place was cold, austere, but it was now his hurricane home. The atmosphere didn't matter. The only home on his mind was in Holgate, and it would be staring Sandy straight in the eye come tomorrow.

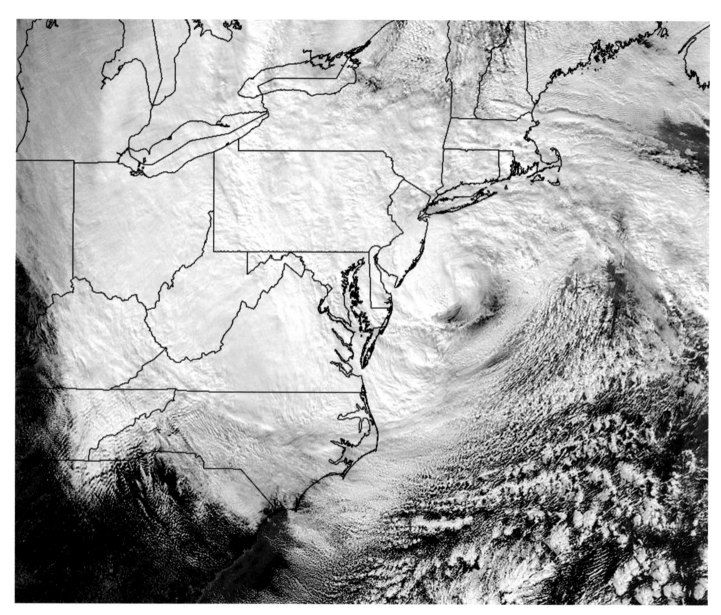

Visible satellite image just before landfall: NASA's Aqua satellite captured Sandy's massive circulation on October 29 at 2:20 p.m. EDT. The superstorm covers 1.8 million square miles, from the Mid-Atlantic to the Ohio Valley, into Canada and New England.

MONDAY, OCTOBER 29, 2012:

Direct Hit

CHAPTER SIX

The Weather is Here

Overnight the northeast wind pushed water south from Barnegat Bay, and by dawn on Monday, October 29, Little Egg Harbor was already overflowing. All that water was being trapped by more water surging in through the inlets and the sedge islands. The water then forced its way over bulkheads all over the Island, sending it into the yards and streets under the cloak of night.

On most streets, there was little evidence of urgency. Barbeque and outdoor furniture sat in backyards and on decks, kayaks leaned against houses. Few windows were boarded up, although some had the last-minute addition of a quick spread of a taped "X".

Down in Holgate, Charlie Potter woke up to water already filling some of the side streets and parts of his yard. To see the water this high this early was a surprise. The hurricane wasn't supposed to make landfall until that evening. He got dressed and took a walk around the neighborhood to check on friends and to see what else was happening. A few blocks away the ocean was already up to the beachfront pavilion at the end of Washington Avenue. The sea looked like a cauldron of energy ready to boil over. The pavilion is built on top of a steep dune, and even though it's relatively high up, waves already washed up and around it. Potter ran into Don Kartan, who lives around the corner at Farreny's RV Park. Kartan said he was concerned about water making its way up from the bayside and from the end of West Street.

Potter went back to the house. By 9 a.m. the water had risen so quickly that he knew it was going to get into the house — and soon. Potter raced to put the most important items as high up as he could get them — a scene playing out in homes all over the Island and in bay towns on the Mainland. Potter cared

deeply for an antique desk, a family heirloom, so he put that as high up on the couch as he could get it.

The water just kept coming. Soon it reached the steps, then to the thresholds. Here we go, Potter thought, as water entered the house. As high tide arrived it brought two inches of water to every room. Realizing his son's toys were still scattered in the yard, Potter went outside to grab them. He stumbled a few times on objects under the surface. Even after the peak of high tide, the water did not ebb. It was staying and there was more coming.

By 11:30 a.m., Potter began wondering if he could ride out the storm. *The first high tide is never the worst*, he thought. *The next high tide is going to be bad*. He decided to leave. Many of his belongings and even his jugs of freshwater were already under saltwater. He grabbed his bag and left the house. *You just have to trust your gut and go with what you think. Where I'm heading is safer than where I'm coming from*. The Sea Shell would have the food and cases of freshwater he needed.

So he began his trek to Beach Haven, two miles to the north. He knew friends and coworkers were riding out the storm at the Shell, so his plan was to head there — on foot. He sloshed through his flooded yard and headed up Roosevelt Avenue to Long Beach Boulevard. Strangely, despite water being

Evacuation was no longer an option when flooding made access to the Causeway impossible at the Ship Bottom circle (above); at left, the Boulevard in Surf City.

relatively deep in the yard, there were spots on the Boulevard that had no water at all, while other areas had more than six inches in spots.

He walked north up the Boulevard and made it about four and a half blocks when he noticed water rushing over the boulevard between Jacqueline and Carolina avenues. It was ocean water. Sandy's initial high tide had completely eroded the dune between two oceanfront homes. There was nothing between the ocean and the Boulevard through that 10-foot-wide cut. He took a couple of photographs on his phone as the ocean water streamed onto the Boulevard and across the street toward Hurley's Motel and the homes behind it. The water coming through the breach rushed through as waves broke, but brief breaks between waves allowed him to cross safely.

There some more breaches along the way, but the dune line held its ground fairly well and Potter made his way to Liberty Avenue, about a mile north of his house, where a National Guard truck loaded with more people from Holgate picked him up. The truck was heading back to Beach Haven and must have missed Potter on its way south as it traversed the side streets. Potter's boulevard

journey had come to an end. He made it to the Sea Shell Resort by noon.

☙

The Edwin B. Forsythe National Wildlife Refuge is a wilderness area, part of which encompasses the entire southern tip of Long Beach Island. The refuge is about a mile long and protects the beach in its purest, most natural and unaltered form. It also provides a natural refuge and breeding grounds for wildlife, especially shorebirds like the piping plover. For decades the human element on the refuge has been limited to seasonal sport fishing and the occasional surfer or beach hiker. In the warm weather months the refuge is closed to the public altogether. While the rest of the Island beaches have been modified by artificial attempts at controlling beach erosion, the refuge has been left unspoiled and untouched, aside from some protective fencing and a few U.S. Fish and Wildlife Service signs. The lack of jetties has allowed the southern end of the Island to behave like a natural barrier island. The sand migrates west as the beach ebbs and flows in a cycle of dune erosion and natural rehabilitation that continues on and on as the entire spit of land cycles

In Beach Haven, at the Sea Shell Hotel, the ocean surges over the dunes and onto the streets.

towards the Mainland.

West Avenue runs parallel to the west of Long Beach Boulevard in southern Holgate. It ends at the wildlife refuge, about 300 feet from the ocean beach. Two and half blocks north, Don and Clarice Kartan lived in a 32-foot Starcraft mobile home in Farreny's Family RV Park and Boat Basin. Don, a carpenter by trade, and Clarice, who runs an online business selling art and natural recycled crafts, had a lot perpendicular to West Avenue, about halfway between Washington and McKinley avenues. Their home was set close to the street, slightly lower in elevation than the rest of the trailer park, with about twenty neighboring mobile homes between their home and the bay. Farreny's RV Park was known to boaters in the area for the homemade submarine that sat dry-docked along its bayfront. To the west of the submarine, dozens of boat slips jut out into Little Egg Harbor. Farenny's land was built on fill and purposely sits at a slightly higher elevation than West Avenue. Being near the street, though, the Kartans' home was just a little lower than the others.

As Charlie Potter dealt with water coming into his house, the Kartans watched the ocean begin to fill the side streets and West Avenue. By mid-morning it was thigh high. They now faced a situation they thought was only an outside possibility the day before. Should they take their chances in the RV or flee to the neighbor's home? With water quickly flowing down the streets, the latter choice was the only choice. They grabbed the bags they had prepared, and their pets, and headed to the neighbor's house directly across the street.

Once there, Don and Clarice waited for the storm to arrive. As water continued to envelop the streets, they took it upon themselves to become the local neighborhood watch. Don waded around to check on his neighbors, including the Bowkers at the deli just up McKinley Avenue. Eventually the water started to flow too quickly to safely walk through, and Don headed back.

A little over two miles north in Beach Haven, Mark Cohen looked out the window at water outside. Everywhere. He and his brother Craig own the Chicken or the Egg, a popular restaurant in the heart of town. Cohen felt the same about Sandy as many other business owners in town. He was skeptical.

In Ship Bottom, at the circle, a small boat offered the only way to move for patrolmen Brian Tretola, Ron Holloway and Sergeant Scott Barr (left). In between answering calls the police officers played a game called "name the floating object" — for example, "basketball or pumpkin?" At right, the docks in Barnegat Light.

The surging ocean cuts through the dunes, under a house, and pours across the Island toward the bay.

On Bay Avenue in the middle of Beach Haven, the sign for the Chicken or Egg illuminates the rising flood waters.

The evacuation prior to Hurricane Irene the weekend before Labor Day in 2012 had cost businesses up and down the Island a lot of money. And then Irene fizzled. The Cohens had kept the restaurant open as long as possible, but shut things down by Sunday. Once the evacuation deadline hit at 4 p.m., all Cohen could do was wait it out with his wife and daughter at their home, a short walk away.

Cohen wasn't expecting to wake up to such severe flooding. The family car was half under water. Sandy was clearly no Irene.

His first order of business was to figure out a way to get his wife, daughter and their dog and cat to safety. He called a friend who was a first responder in town and arranged to be taken to the Engleside Inn. Borough authorities were urging anyone who needed to leave their home to seek shelter there. The first responders did not arrive in fire trucks or sport utility vehicles — they arrived on jet skis. His wife, daughter and pets were loaded up and taken away. Cohen waited for a ride. A bit later he boarded the Beach Haven Volunteer Fire Company's ex-military "deuce" vehicle. When he arrived at the Engleside, he saw it wasn't just the rescued that were taking up residence. It looked like the entire first responder force was there. Fire engines, a tower truck, command and support SUVs, and the water rescue vehicle with the jet skies crammed the Engleside parking lot and parts of Bicentennial Park across the street. The

Surf and sea foam washes over the dunes, past homes, toward the Boulevard and bay in North Beach.

firehouse on the corner of Amber and Bay avenues was already flooding. That much was expected. Heavy downpours or extreme tides often sent water into the Boulevard and side streets around the firehouse, and it's standard practice for the department to move all apparatus and vital equipment to the Engleside Inn when a storm approaches.

The hotel is known as a haven in storms, sitting high above South Atlantic Avenue and the Victorian section of town. Guests are taken care of and a generator provides power throughout any crisis. Careful planning by the hotel's owners after the '62 Storm helped ensure that. After the historic three-day northeaster the owners built a 30-foot wall perpendicular to the sea, using piling plunged deep into the sand on the ocean side of the hotel. The wall, almost totally covered by dune, has made the Engleside a virtual fortress at the east end of Engleside Avenue and Amber Street.

The Cohens joined other evacuees, first responders and hotel owner John Hillman's brother, sister and mother, who were also staying there during the storm. As a staging area for the first responders, evacuees, and those seeking refuge, it didn't take long for the rooms to fill up. As Beach Haven began to flood in earnest, more and more people fled to the yellow beachfront hotel.

Cohen's thoughts shifted to his restaurant. After what he had seen outside of his house and on the ride to the hotel, he was not optimistic. Someone had posted a photograph of the Chicken or the Egg on Facebook during the night. Cohen looked at it on his cell phone. The photograph showed water already up to the windows, but the neon sign was still bright and inviting, as it would be on any typical Monday night in October. The photograph brought an eerie mix of hope and hopelessness.

One mile north, Angela Andersen watched the water cover her driveway on Waverly Place in North Beach Haven. The last time she witnessed a scene like this was in the December '92 northeaster. "Well, it's here!" she shouted to her family. Landfall was actually hours away but the water was making its way closer and closer. Soon it was two feet high. Then three. Her husband, Jim, secured as much as possible in the yard and began working on the garage, hoping to get the important stuff higher than the water. After the garage was secured, they turned their attention to the interior of the house. They moved whatever they could get up the stairwell upstairs. Higher and higher the water rose, and soon it flowed over the deck. Then it entered the interior porch. It was time to go.

The Andersen family is not prone to panic. The family stayed because it is their home. If they left, there was no guarantee they would be allowed back. Angela Andersen is the recycling coordinator for Long Beach Township and she knew her decision to stay wouldn't go over well at the township's Office of Emergency Management.

The Andersens purchased the house in 1994 from Jim's grandfather, a pound fisherman in Barnegat Light. The core of the home dates back to 1944. After Jim's family lost a home in Holgate to the Hurricane of '44, they purchased the one on Waverly. That was the second home they lost to a storm. He had the home on Waverly placed on extra long piling in an effort to avoid losing another one. Now water was threatening to get in the house. The house wasn't in danger of floating off its foundation, but it was going to flood, at least on the first floor.

The Andersen children — Liam, 11, and Nolan, 9 — weren't scared. The water run up was fast, but not intense. The Andersens didn't feel like they were in any danger, but they knew it was time to head to the house a neighbor on 14th Street had offered.

Jim Andersen got everyone into a rowboat. Although the water was relatively calm in the driveway, it was moving enough to need a boat. Waves would make walking difficult, especially with kids. So Jim tied a rope around his waist and pulled his family to the neighbor's house. It wasn't far, and they made it without difficulty. On the way they caught a clean view of the whitecap-covered bay.

As they settled into their temporary home, Angela thought about the other house she was put in charge of. Her father had asked her to prepare the family beach house for the storm. The oceanfront home was located on 80th Street in Beach Haven Crest. The flooding around her house on Waverly was bay flooding, but the way the ocean was churned up, she feared that her parents' home was vulnerable to the storm surge. She had no way to tell how it was faring.

At daybreak in Ship Bottom, the floodwaters had not been much of a concern, but now, only a few hours later, they were nearing or exceeding levels reached in the 1992 northeaster. Water gushed out of manhole covers. Expected landfall was still half a day away.

The phones at Ship Bottom's police dispatch were lighting up with calls from nervous residents who stayed. Patrolmen radioed that some were shouting for help from open windows and doors, their homes surrounded by water. They manned a motorized 14-foot flat-bottom aluminum fishing boat, owned by one of the officers, to reach people in flooded out areas. The boat was small and could only hold a handful of people.

Conditions grew more difficult by the hour, making the small boat difficult to manage. Patrolman Brian Tretola was tossed off the boat on one run. He maintained a grip on the boat and was able to get back in with the help of Patrolman Ron Holloway and Sergeant Scott Barr. They pressed on. The same officers came across a woman trapped in her car. Frozen with fear and sitting in a car half filled with seawater, her fingers gripped the steering wheel so hard they had to be pried off.

They didn't stop until conditions became too dangerous. In all, the officers rescued forty residents using the small boat.

Some didn't wait for first responders. The Perry family wanted to leave, but shelters on the Mainland would not take their pets. They decided to take matters into their own hands. After scoping out the yard and surrounding area for a way out, Ken Perry piled everyone into their old Ford pickup truck and made his way through the floodwaters. He barely made it over a berm to get to 9th Street where he took a chance driving westbound on the eastbound lanes. He managed to get the truck over to the appropriate lanes by crossing the

parking lot of the old Country Corner Farm Market. Once on Route 72, they followed National Guard vehicles over the causeway bridges and headed to a relative's home in Moorestown.

Meanwhile, another Ship Bottom resident, Pete Pianetti, stared at a big problem outside his one-story home on 9th Street. He had spent Sunday preparing for the storm at East Coast Auto Repair, a shop he had owned for a little more than two months. He had put his most valuable tools and toolbox on the lift, hoping to prevent damage from flooding, and decided to ride the storm out in his house across from the shop. His fiancée, Michelle, couldn't get back on the Island Sunday night. By Monday morning he realized that he might have a problem. Now he was thinking he might have to move to the attic. Then his friend, Randy Townsend, called and invited him to ride out the storm at his place in Surf City.

Pianetti put on his wetsuit and headed out to his truck. He carefully drove through the floodwaters across the street to Ron Jon's Surf Shop. The water was too deep, so he continued on across the street to the parking lot of the Lyceum gym. He parked the truck and looked around. Water surrounded the lot. He grabbed his backpack and started walking on Barnegat Avenue. It was chest-high. Although no one was around, he felt like an idiot being out in this mess. And walking was a lot harder than he expected. Exhausted, fourteen blocks later, he walked into Townsend's house.

Nestled in the dunes of Barnegat Light, a house sat vacant. It overlooks Barnegat Inlet and Barnegat Light's massive beaches. David Kaltenbach climbed the steps to the highest deck of the house. He figured the home's owner, a friend of his, wouldn't mind. Kaltenbach has been a Long Beach Island resident for 50 years. He has lived in Barnegat Light for the last ten. An avid videographer, he stayed on the Island to document the storm. He made it to the top deck and scanned the area. It was 11 a.m. and water covered the massive south jetty.

It was a sight Kaltenbach had never witnessed before. He looked again — sure enough, the ocean was submerging the 4,290-foot-long inlet jetty. The installation of the south jetty in 1991 helped to stabilize the shifting sands of the inlet. The project increased the size of borough beaches and land within Barnegat Lighthouse State Park dramatically. The new beaches are so wide that beachgoers need a tram to take them to the water. Kaltenbach looked over the windswept beaches and wondered if they were wide enough.

Surf City police and public works employees wade into the storm for a rescue.

CHAPTER SEVEN

Monday, Monday

The view of Long Beach Boulevard at Jacqueline Avenue in Holgate as the sea raged through the dunes (above). At right, the Boat House Restaurant and the Ketch on Dock Road in Beach Haven during the storm surge Monday night.

Water rushed down Long Beach Boulevard in front of Island Surf & Sail in Brant Beach, but Jack Bushko was determined to cross. *This is nothing, just keep an eye on the debris floating in there*, he thought. Bushko has stayed on the Island for every tropical weather event for just shy of three decades. A water sports instructor at Island Surf & Sail, he's windsurfed or tackled previous storms in one way or another without a problem. Heck, he once drove a jet ski down the Boulevard in a flood like this. Dry-suited up, he walked into the road. The waist-deep water flowed around him. He could feel it tugging at him, threatening to pull him down. But he kept upright, and just like that he was on the other side, out of the tumult.

It had been that kind of Monday for Bushko. Of course the storm had to hit while he was between rentals. His new place was supposed to be ready November 1. He had been staying in the apartment above the water sports shop. That morning Bushko watched as water flooded into the store at high tide, quickly rising to about 18 inches. After a frantic burst of placing as much up as high as possible, the water receded a bit. But not for long. Less than an hour later, a new surge flooded the store, and this one meant business. Water found its way through crawlspaces and floorboards. It made its way around the entire building. Bushko heard the sound of paddleboards, kayaks and debris banging around.

The store filled up so fast Bushko had put on a dry suit and grabbed a rescue air can and headed upstairs. The living room was only four steps higher than the store, so he had to go up to the true second floor, which housed the bedrooms. The flooding was so intense he thought for a while he'd have to

jump to safety from the bedroom-level deck. Not necessary. When things calmed down a bit, Bushko decided to head to the beach.

He could feel the pit in his stomach growing. He had been uneasy ever since Sandy began its westward trek toward the Jersey Shore. Bushko walked up 33rd Street to the beach ramp, a vantage point he'd looked out from a million times. Now it seemed unfamiliar. Scanning the horizon, all he could see was white water and gray clouds. He estimated the waves at about thirty feet. They were breaking higher than the dune he was standing on. His apprehension ratcheted up to actual fear. The storm was not only coming, it was bringing the whole ocean with it.

A mile and a half south, local business owner and resident Stephen DiPietro and his friend Jim Leonetti dodged around the flooded streets in a small Toyota sport utility. DiPietro had spent the early afternoon checking the flooding near his restaurant on 19th Street and around Beach Haven Terrace and Haven Beach. Now word was spreading that there were dune breaches during the first high tide, so the two headed up to 112th Street in Haven Beach to check.

They parked the vehicle and headed toward the beach. As they approached, a wave broke over the dune. The sea had already eaten away much of the walkway on the ocean side.

"Oh, this is trouble," DiPietro said. "Oh wow, that's something I've never seen before." Water came over the dune and washed down towards them. DiPietro immediately took out his cell phone and started narrating while taping.

"Here we are at 112th Street and the ocean's coming over … Holy schmoly! Holy… Jimmy!" he shouted. Sand-muddied waves pushed their way up and over what was left of the wooded beach ramp and forcefully flowed down the remaining dune and to the street, pulling at DiPietro's feet.

They watched in amazement at the sheer volume of water making its way up and over the dune. Every thirty seconds a new wave sent more whitewater into the street. It was time to head to higher ground. Sandy was breaching dunes all over the Island, infiltrating the roadways, making some impassable — all in less than the half hour from the time DiPietro had parked.

DiPietro needed a place to ride out the storm. A friend owned an oceanfront home nearby, but he dismissed that because it was a Cape, and after seeing the surf rip the dune apart, he didn't like its chances. He decided instead to head to his friend Dr. Joseph Lattanzi's house. Lattanzi is a commissioner in Long Beach Township and has a house on Kentucky Avenue in Haven Beach that has

The ocean surges into Holgate at Jacqueline Avenue and Long Beach Boulevard (above). At right, a view of the Boat House restaurant, toward the bay from the New Jersey Maritime Museum in Beach Haven on Monday afternoon, and the Boulevard in Spray Beach.

plenty of room between the floor and the ground. Besides, that meant DiPietro would be with someone with inside knowledge of what was going on.

Skip Carey had wanted to leave the Island. He, his wife Trisha, and their 22-year-old son, Patrick, had a chance Sunday night. Friends offered a place off the Island, but with two huge dogs — both Great Pyrenees-collie mixes — they figured they would hang out in Ship Bottom until morning and burden their friends one less night. But when they tried to leave at about 8 a.m., it was already too late. They couldn't get onto Barnegat Avenue. Central Avenue was the other option, but the water there was already thigh high. There was no way out.

All day the water came up 5th Street. Never in the twenty-six years the Careys lived on the Island had water made it up their street. Yet Skip watched as the ocean met the bay in front of their house, between Barnegat and Central avenues.

Water came up the driveway and into the garage. Out front, power lines swayed in the wind. A transformer exploded. The wire blew off the pole

and fell to the water below, where it continued to spark beneath the surface. Trisha immediately phoned the borough to report the downed, sparking wire.

Trisha was already nervous about the storm. Now a live wire might be feeding who-knows-what-kind of voltage into the water that was flooding the garage. The garage sat lower than the house and contained the water heater, furnace and their storage. Patrick opened the garage door. Stuff was already floating around. As he raised his foot to step into the water, Skip pulled him back from the threshold, warning him of possible current from the downed power line.

Skip also noticed bubbling in the street outside, about fifteen feet from the submerged wire. A natural gas main under a manhole cover appeared to be leaking. Now they faced two threats — electrocution and explosion. The National Guard pulled up in a large truck and surveyed the situation, but there was nothing they could do. They signaled as much to the family.

The Careys watched as the water rose up the porch steps, hoping it would not reach the main house. They could hear transformers popping all over town. Eventually power went out. They actually felt relieved. It had solved the problem of the downed power line.

☻

On 84th Street in the Brighton Beach section of Long Beach Township, Zach Kerzner

was in pain. He hurt his back in a recent paddleboard mishap. Now he felt it every time he moved. And he had to make a major move. Kerzner had watched the water rise over the top of his deck and start entering the house. He glanced down at Ruby, his trusty pooch. It was going to be just the two of them. The cat, Alley Cat, would have to tough it out in the house while he and Ruby tried to make it to the Mainland.

Ruby is Kerzner's support system, a rescue dog from the streets of Louisiana, tough as nails and loyal as can be. She and Kerzner ventured outside. They made their way down the flooded street to Beach Avenue, Ruby swimming part of the way, to the yard where Kerzner had parked his two trucks. He took one and headed north to the Long Beach Township Municipal Complex. The dunes had held up along this stretch of road, even as it turned into Ocean Boulevard in Brant Beach. He pulled into the eastern parking lot of the complex and parked.

Kerzner and Ruby went into the township meeting hall and simply waited it out. Mayor Joseph Mancini, Commissioner Joseph

The tide kept rising on Monday — inside the New Jersey Maritime Museum on Dock Road in Beach Haven (above) and at 33rd Street and the Boulevard in Brant Beach (right).

Lattanzi, Police Chief Michael Bradley, and Police Captain Anthony Deely rushed in and out of the room, busy running township operations. Ruby played with Lattanzi's dog.

Kerzner looked around. *Why didn't I make sure I got off the Island yesterday? This is just silly.* He knew the answer. The pain medication left him unable to drive. The plan was to go to bed early and hit the road early. But when he woke the Boulevard was already flooded. Now he was stuck waiting for a ride to the Mainland.

More familiar faces showed up, including his good friend, Don Tracy, who owned Bay Haven Marina. He had jet skied to his truck, which he had also parked on Beach Avenue. In mid-afternoon their ride arrived. The township was using a refurbished school bus to patrol and rescue citizens. It would take them to Ship Bottom.

Kerzner just wanted to get off the Island. Looking out the bus windows, he saw nothing but flooded streets and a whole lot of misery for people coming back after the storm. Sparks of pain shot through his body. The suspension on the old school bus wasn't helping. At least Ruby was taking it all in stride. She just wanted off the Island too.

They arrived at the Ship Bottom Borough Hall and waited for a while until a National Guard vehicle pulled up and dropped off passengers, among them Ship Bottom Mayor William Huelsenbeck and a group of local officials. Kerzner, Ruby, Tracy and the rest got

Storm-churned foam foreshadows the oncoming surge on the northbound lane of Long Beach Boulevard in North Beach (above). Chest waders or wetsuits were the necessary beachwear on Monday.

on. Kerzner could barely walk at this point, so a National Guardsman picked up Ruby and put her in the back of the truck. Then he helped Kerzner get in.

On the bridges, winds gusting to 70 mph rocked the truck. Kerzner thought about storms he had seen come and go in his 40 years on the Island. This was the first that worried him. He was glad to be heading off.

Surf City Fire Chief Peter Hartney watched as the bay tides reached Central Avenue. The firehouse was getting call after call from people needing rescue. Ed and Ann Marie Hoffman had tried to leave by car but only got as far as Ron Jon's in Ship Bottom before they met a roadblock. The Causeway was flooded. A car sat abandoned in the water ahead. They decided to go back to their home on 20th Street. Soon after, they got a call from their friend, Andy Warren, who worked for the borough. He picked them up and they headed to the Surf City firehouse.

All day Monday, crews drove heavy trucks to rescue residents. As the flooding worsened, Hartney instructed those crews to go as far as they could in trucks then walk down to the houses and put the people in boats.

Like the Hoffmans, everyone ended up at the firehouse, where they enjoyed some semblance of calm and a heap of hospitality from the volunteers and first responders. The firehouse was also a staging area for people waiting for a National Guard ride to the Mainland.

The Hoffmans and a group of about three-dozen evacuees crammed in the back of one National Guard truck at around 5 p.m. Ed was one of the last ones on and had to stand and hold onto the top rail. The canvas top billowed wildly in the wind as the truck crossed the first of the bridges leaving the Island. The rear flap flew open. The Island he saw out of the back of the truck was almost unrecognizable. Only houses and trees provided enough familiarity to gain his bearings. Then, by shear luck, he caught a glimpse of the iconic Shack. Only a wall or two was still standing. And as Hoffman watched, it just fell over. He couldn't believe it — he watched the Shack disappear. He turned to the other evacuees. "The Shack is gone! The Shack is *gone*!" he said. The group cheered.

Lloyd Vosseller has worked in the Harvey Cedars Public Works Department for thirty-six years. Now superintendent, he stayed in town as Sandy rolled in. He is also an avid weather buff who maintains a website filled with detailed real-time weather readings and archived data. Vosseller saw something different in Sandy. Never had a hurricane come straight at us from the east, from the ocean. They always go north and skirt us. Long Island gets the straight shots.

Vosseller drove a borough tractor onto the beach entrance on Middlesex Avenue. Above the clatter of the engine he heard the shrill rasp of the wind gusts as they pelted his face. The streets are graded up from the Boulevard in Harvey Cedars to act as a secondary dune line. The houses east of the main road are, on average,

An evacuation truck plows through the tide on the Boulevard in Surf City (above). At left, a final view of the Causeway shack from an evacuation vehicle, just before it collapsed.

eight feet higher than the rest of the town. The elevation offered Vosseller a good vantage point from which to check the beach.

A restoration project recently created massive beaches that Vosseller felt confident could handle the onslaught of the storm. When the Army Corps of Engineers designed the beach project, it put the primary dune farther to the east, with a flatter area to the west of it to absorb the tidal surge. Vosseller could see that the core dune was now disappearing and the ocean was starting to overwash what was left, filling the flat area behind it.

Meanwhile, down in Holgate, the dunes had already lost their battle. On Jacqueline Avenue, Marilyn Howard watched the same dune break Charlie Potter passed a few hours earlier. Water had been gushing through the breach all day while more and more of the dune on both sides eroded with each

passing hour. Now a river ran down the street past their house and on toward the bay. Large flowerpots floated by with flowers still in them. Garbage can corrals, staircases and mailboxes followed. And the water just kept coming.

The Howards retired here in 2004. They purchased the property back in the 1990s as a seasonal getaway. The original home was a small ranch built on a concrete slab. No piling, no height to speak of — just a slab. Wanting a more substantial year-round home, they replaced the ranch with a house that sits high atop piling, with wrap-around decks and a brick paver driveway. They were confident they could weather the storm. They had a generator wired to their home after Hurricane Irene and their gas fireplace provided heat even without power.

Marilyn heard a loud bang in the foyer on the bottom floor of the house. A wave knocked in the front doors. Water rushed into the foyer. Her husband Buzz tried to close the doors, but the power of the water was too much.

They had taken as much as they could upstairs, but many things in the garage and workroom were too big or not moveable. When the doors went, the power of the rushing water ripped away anything that would budge. With his jeans wet and hard to walk in, Buzz took them off. After nearly being swept away in his underwear, Buzz gave up and went upstairs. Looking down, their interior staircase descended into a cold, whirling pool of saltwater.

Seven blocks to the south, dune breaks combined with a flooded bay sent ocean and bay water gushing onto the back streets, putting the southern end of West Avenue and parts of McKinley and Washington avenues under three feet of water.

Eileen Bowker watched. She was concerned, and growing more so by the minute. As she looked out the window, a massive wave broke over the top of the bathhouse that sits behind a massive dune in the municipal parking lot. Their home is only a stone's throw away. Even though they're on the second floor, Eileen considered the odds. She remembered the offer from her neighbor, Dave Allerie.

With large waves breaking near the deli, it was time to make a decision. Eileen asked if they should move to higher ground. Brian told her they should look for a sign. Then, with amazing timing, a massive wave sent the entire bathhouse careening down McKinley Avenue and into a resident's yard. It was more than enough to convince them.

They had prepared for this. The bags were packed and in dry bags. They put on the wetsuits and headed out into the heart of the storm. Carefully, they went down the outside stairs. The kayaks lashed to the piling floated in shallow water. They untied one and put the dry bags and their massive dog, Otis, on top. The ocean had broken the dune line across the street and ripped apart the garage areas under the oceanfront homes. With three feet of water rushing down the Boulevard, they decided to slog it out by walking through the tree line that separates the neighbors' yards.

What normally would be a couple-minute walk became a drawn-out, harrowing experience as they trudged through deeper and deeper water. They saw waves breaking close by on Washington Avenue. Soaked with wind-swept rain, they forged through the yards and floating debris, navigating their cargo and canine-laden kayak. It took almost thirty minutes to get to Allerie's house. By the time they reached the steps the water was chest-deep. But they made it.

Just up the road, the Kartans watched the sea envelop their trailer home on the other side of the street. The dunes at the wildlife refuge had also breached and water flowed over the refuge and up West Avenue, where it met equally rapid water rushing from the ocean up Washington Avenue. The house the Kartans took refuge in was high and avoided flooding. Their mobile home, vacated, sat on its three-foot base, perched precariously over the rapidly rising water on West Avenue.

Either a utility pole or a loose piling barreled into the deck on the side of the house. Don knew it could rip the entire deck off if it kept slamming, leaving them no way out. They would be trapped. Don walked into the mud-colored abys, grabbed the piling and shoved it away from the house. He looked around. Water covered yards and debris floated everywhere.

Don spent the remainder of the afternoon in waist-high water pushing debris away from the house and up West Avenue. When a 15-foot deck slowly floated by, heading straight toward their trailer, he wrestled the deck by hand and diverted it around. Everything they owned was inside. It was bad enough watching water damage the outside of the trailer. He wasn't going to watch a deck slam into it and lose all of its contents.

Less than half a mile north, Carl and Susan Clark had gathered yard ornaments, bird feeders and wind chimes from around their home on the corner of Bay Terrace and Carolina Avenue. They brought in the flowerpots on the deck railings and everything else they could carry. They tied down second-floor deck chairs, the gas grill and garbage cans. That's when they noticed the water getting deeper and the rain falling harder.

Sue worried about her rose bushes. After purchasing their home in the fall of 1996, Carl and Susan Clark marked the passing of each summer season by planting a new rose bush in their yard. Their grandchildren loved coming to Holgate during the summers, and the traditional planting of the rose bush took on more meaning through the years. The roses in the yard grew a little more vibrant when the Clarks made the beach house their permanent residence in 2009.

As evening approached, an unexpected visitor wandered to their sliding glass doors and begged to come in. It was a feral kitten. The Clarks had seen the brood this cat belonged to over the years. Feral cats are common in Holgate, but this one practically knocked at the door in the middle of a storm. Carl raced off and grabbed a large cat carrier and Susan found a thick fluffy towel to stuff in it. They opened the slider a few inches and the kitten jumped right in — exhausted but happy to be inside.

Carl and Susan moved to the second floor as water began rising up over the decking. They feared water might seep up through the floorboards on the first floor. The yard was no longer their principal worry. Just getting through the storm was.

Looking south on the Boulevard from Surf City toward the Ship Bottom circle (above); at left, Surf City.

CHAPTER EIGHT

Landfall

When Charlie Potter arrived at the Shell in Beach Haven at around noon, the area was still in good shape. Bicentennial Park was untouched and the properties of both hotels looked relatively normal — aside from the firefighting apparatus parked in the Engleside parking lot. Potter's truck remained safe in the Shell's western parking lot. The only evidence a hurricane was on its way was at the beach. It was taking a pounding.

Walking into the main dining room and bar area, wooden boards blacked out the wall of glass windows behind the big oak bar that look out over a pool and the Shell's trademark tiki bars. Aside from the wind, the blowing sand and the forecast, things felt secure. At least more secure than his flooded house in Holgate.

But the feeling would be fleeting. Sitting at the darkened bar, the wind whistled as it blew against the boards covering the windows, Potter began to realize it was only a matter of time.

Tom Hughes, the owner of the Sea Shell since 1992, was not terribly worried about flooding. Historically, it stayed dry in storms. When his father owned it, he didn't even have flood insurance. He figured if it ever did flood, he'd just open the front doors and let the water go through. Hughes left directions to have the electric turned off to avoid a fire. While off the Island, he asked anyone still at the hotel on Monday to "abandon ship." Only one man was expected to stay and his job was to watch the roof, which had a precarious drainage system. Hughes wanted early warning if that were to go.

But his employees did not close the hotel. They called Hughes at home and told him residents were coming by looking for a room. The Engleside was full so they gravitated to the hotel across the street, even if it was not officially open. Hughes knew he could not turn them away. He told his employees to let them in, but to keep the electricity off. But the workers only shut off the electricity downstairs — or so they thought.

Potter and bartender Willy Logue tried to direct the electrical breakers in the building to only send power where it was needed, and where it was safe. They spent about an hour searching for breaker boxes so they could shut off nonessential circuits before the water found them.

Then a wave dislodged a door and sent water into the pool utility room, which shares a wall with one of the inside bars. The wall couldn't hold back the water and it began flowing in behind the beer cooler.

Realizing the water was now reaching electrical sockets in the building, Potter and Logue tried to shut off as many circuits to the bar as they could find. They thought they had them all, but they still heard fans to the beer coolers running. Making matters worse, the motors started smoking. Hoping to avoid a fire, they unplugged the coolers. They were heavy — about 350 pounds empty and they were still stocked for the fishing tournament with about a dozen cases of beer. Potter got behind the bar, pushed out the smaller of the two coolers and unplugged it. He couldn't budge the large one. He asked Logue for help.

As they gripped the cooler, a loud, thunderous crack stopped them cold. In a rapid chain reaction, a massive wave snapped the dividers between the boarded-up windows and wall of the bar. Floor to ceiling, 120 feet of windows crashed in on the ocean side of the wall. Water swept up debris, the remnants of the wall, the side of the bar, the beer cooler. And the two men. They careened into the other side of the bar. The bar broke in half and, along with the cooler, trapped both of the bartender's feet and pinned Potter's ankle. They couldn't move the cooler and they couldn't free their legs. Potter tried to shove the bar top away with his free leg, but couldn't.

They yelled for help. Another Shell employee heard them. He rushed into the room but could not budge the beer coolers. He ran across the street, through rushing water, to get help from firefighters stationed at the Engleside Inn. Within a few minutes, firefighters and some local residents showed up. Charlie asked that they get Logue out first. As they attempted to free his friend, the cooler trapping Potter pressed harder against his ankle. It hurt so much Potter at one point suggested cutting the foot off. That wasn't necessary. The

Rapids can be seen as the sea attempts to create a new inlet in Holgate with a torrent of storm surge. This washover from the beach crosses the Island and empties into the bay at the end of Carolina Avenue. Later that evening, an entire house will float from the east end of Carolina Avenue to this very spot, dragging a sport utility vehicle with it. The house remained here until it was torn down in August 2013.

In Holgate the dunes vanish and homes stand in the surf.

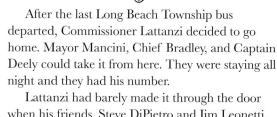

After the last Long Beach Township bus departed, Commissioner Lattanzi decided to go home. Mayor Mancini, Chief Bradley, and Captain Deely could take it from here. They were staying all night and they had his number.

Lattanzi had barely made it through the door when his friends, Steve DiPietro and Jim Leonetti, arrived. He and his wife, Kim, invited DiPietro and Leonetti in and offered them a bite to eat and a chance to dry off. DiPietro told them about the breach in the dunes and how the sand was filling the streets. He couldn't get home, which is why he stopped by.

As it got dark, the small gathering grew into an impromptu hurricane get-together. In-laws, friends, as well as their dogs, all made their way in. Soon it was a party of ten. Time to try to relax, enjoy the company, and make the best of a bad situation.

The group went outside to a pleasant surprise — the wind had died considerably. They stayed out watching the water churn below them. Time passed and the moon came out.

The calmness belied Sandy's impending storm surge. As the group relaxed upstairs, the dunes gave up their final hold on the beachfront. The ocean broke through, breaching at every street end. Within minutes, the water rose rapidly around the house.

men were able to get Potter's leg free. He was fine — bruised and numb, but able to walk away.

When they opened the front doors, water rushed out and took virtually everything with it. The entire inside was completely gone. All the bars were destroyed, the kitchens, the meeting rooms, floors, everything.

Potter went upstairs and got his stuff. The Shell didn't seem too stable anymore. About a dozen people filed out of the hotel, crossed the river of ocean water to the safety of the Engleside.

Across the street the ocean blew out the garage doors of an old Cape Cod, spewing its contents down the street. Lounge chairs, boogie boards and garbage can receptacles drifted by. No one was certain that the little house would stay on its foundation. The last thing they wanted to see was it careening into the house they were in.

The surge pierced the garages and foyer under Lattanzi's house. Water quickly filled up the garage and foyer level and made its way up, step-by-step, as high as the second step from the top — but stopped short of the living space.

Whipping winds announced Sandy's landfall. The center of the storm

Long Beach Boulevard, Holgate, looking north.

The rising storm tide pours ashore, over the Island's beaches and streets, in torrents.

crossed onto land about 15 miles south. Power lines on the poles outside barely contained their grip on the grid. Transformers sparked with brilliant white-blue-green flashes, the lightning-like bursts lighting up the homes and the floodwaters below, sparks cascading into the whitewater.

At Ship Bottom Borough Hall, Mayor Huelsenbeck watched as police vehicles returned from transporting evacuees to the shelter at Southern Regional High School in Stafford Township. He and Police Chief Paul Sharkey had just stepped outside. They noticed how quiet it had gotten. Huelsenbeck looked up at the flag that sat limp against the pole. No wind, just the sound of the ocean.

That's when they noticed a bright light over the dunes. Huelsenbeck couldn't see the source. They wondered if a ship was in distress just off the beach? He took out his cell phone and called Harvey Cedars to see if they had any distress reports. They had none. Within a minute or so, the source revealed itself. The clouds broke, unveiling a bright full moon.

Huelsenbeck and Sharkey didn't know what to think. They went back inside. Could the worst be over? Had the Island been spared? Huelsenbeck looked out the back window. They had been using a piling that floated into the borough yard as the high water marker. It sat, high and dry.

Out front they saw some swirling clouds as the moon rose above the buildings across the street. Suddenly, a loud roar shattered the stillness. The flag stood up and whipped. A deluge of water barreled down 16th and 17th streets. The surge shattered large plate glass windows in stores along the Boulevard. For an hour it continued. Debris swept east to west, damaging whatever got in its way. Another surge followed. A police officer radioed that the water on the bayside streets rose 18 inches in a couple of minutes. At the Borough Hall it rose 2½ feet in less than 10 minutes. Everyone remaining was forced to leave.

A National Guard truck returned and officials, members of a first aid crew stationed nearby and the remaining evacuees boarded. The truck went north on the Boulevard. Water had reached five feet high around the Verizon store at 14th Street. On the Causeway, Huelsenbeck looked down and saw a large roof and dormer hit the base of the bridge. He figured there had to have been major breakthrough somewhere to the south, but he had no idea how bad it was.

Back in Beach Haven, the firefighters were functioning on adrenaline. The incident at the Shell was the talk of the moment, but that made up only a small part of a very long day. All day they launched rescues throughout Beach Haven, Holgate, North Beach Haven, and as far north as the Acme in Beach Haven Park. Some of the rescues were made on jet skis, manned by the trained rescue swimmers of Station 15 Beach Haven Fire Department Water Rescue. Others were carried out by the department's firefighters in rescue apparatus or in the military-grade half-ton rescue vehicle,

looked up and there it was.

They trudged back to the Engleside on foot. A different group of firefighters found a different route to the call. The building did not burn down, and a couple of stranded people were brought back to the Engleside.

Just after Sandy made landfall, Andy Warren took a ride to see how Surf City was faring. He and the other guys in the Public Works Department were impressed with how the dunes held. The beach replenishment had worked. There was flooding, sure. He had to dump sand at the top of the dunes at the end of a few streets on the north end of town, but things looked relatively good considering Sandy had just made landfall.

Around 10:30 p.m. the wind died a bit, so Warren and a friend decided to go out again. They were driving north on the Boulevard when his cell phone rang. His brother Rich and his wife were checking conditions at the beach up the street from their home on Holly Avenue in Harvey Cedars.

"The ocean is coming over the dunes up here. What does it look like down there?" Rich asked.

Andy told him the Boulevard wasn't badly flooded in Surf City, and Rich said he was going to take a shot at making it through North Beach in their SUV.

Rich was nervous about staying in Harvey Cedars. The brothers knew their history. They remember what happened in '62. The area Rich was standing on turned into an inlet back then. With the replenished beaches eroded away and another high tide coming, Rich only wanted to get out with his wife, Sue, and son, Greg.

"Look, we're out and about, we'll come north to meet ya," Andy told him.

He drove the up the Boulevard to 23rd Street. Foam covered the roadway. When there's foam, water is close by. Warren turned up the street — one of the ones where they had dumped sand earlier. The sand piles were right where they

which made several trips to Holgate.

Well after dark, a rescue call came in to the command center at the Engleside — a report of a structural fire and possible entrapment on North Bay Avenue. Six firefighters jumped into a 1521 Hahn pumper truck and, with lights flashing and sirens blaring, raced out in the height of the storm.

At Atlantic Avenue and 7th Street, a wave hit the truck, stopping it dead in its tracks. The firefighters emptied the pumper's tank to reduce weight and tried pushing as waves broke around them. Eventually, Firefighter Jimmy Bradshaw, who was driving, told the men to leave it. That's when they saw the full moon. Just as they abandoned the truck with as much gear as they could carry, they

Long Beach Boulevard at 5th Street, Surf City (above).

left them. *Where was the water coming from?* he wondered. They drove about two-thirds of the way up the street when out of nowhere a wall of water came over the top of the dunes. The surge was a foot or two high and it rushed down the street. Water started pouring out from underneath the houses on the north side of the street and down the paved driveways.

Andy threw his vehicle in reverse and backed up to the Boulevard. The phone rang again. It was Rich. They were stuck in North Beach. Rich said they would walk the rest of the way.

"Look, stay in your truck," Andy said.

Rich sounded nervous. "No, we can't — we're getting hit with waves, we gotta get out of here, so we're going to start walking south."

Andy put his truck in gear. Water poured down from 24th Street and down from North Beach along the east side of the Boulevard. Propane tanks, shop vacs and furniture rushed by in the torrent of water. *This is starting to get bad*, he thought.

Andy left Surf City. Water flowed on the northbound lanes of the divided

highway. He drove through it but stopped abruptly about two-thirds of the way into North Beach. Tons of debris washed down the road. In the distance, someone waved a flashlight; it was Rich, Sue and Greg. They were only two blocks away and coming toward him. So much water rushed through. A wave knocked Sue off her feet and Greg had to lunge to grab her. But they made it to the truck and jumped in.

Now Andy needed to turn around without going off of the road and getting stuck. Get into any loose sand or dirt and he might not get out. He got the truck around and the southbound lanes came into view. Sort of. The Boulevard had vanished. The headlights offered only limited visibility, and all they could see was water. It just raced across the Boulevard. Wave after wave hit them, each carrying more debris. They made it through North Beach and, at the Surf City border, Andy looked back. *Had Rich called 15 minutes later*, he thought, *there's no way I could have made it through there.*

They got back to the firehouse, went inside and started to take off their boots when the phone rang again. A friend on Central Avenue in Surf City had water rushing through his house and needed to be picked up. Andy put his boots back on.

But when he ventured back out to get into the truck, the exhaust pipe was underwater. Water levels had risen about two feet.

He couldn't believe it. There they were in the center of Surf City — the water too high to drive through. Andy called his friend back and told him the water won this battle. He could not get to him.

Lloyd Vosseller was out on the borough tractor again, checking for damage. He drove up an easement road just south of Cumberland Avenue in Harvey Cedars. The ocean had come through and beaten up the house on the end pretty badly. A red pickup truck sat almost on its side. Lights flashed under the house next door. Another vehicle on its side, although Vosseller couldn't tell what kind it was. He feared somebody might still be in the house, so he made a couple of quick calls — one to the police and one to the guys at the firehouse. Someone would get up there and check it out. He headed back to the public works building.

Vosseller's main job was maintaining the water supply for the town. There are two water pipes, two wells and two water plants in Harvey Cedars — on Salem Avenue and off of 80th Street. Only Salem has backup generator power. If power went out, Vosseller had an arrangement with Barnegat Light to use some of their water.

That had happened at landfall. Now Vosseller had to meet someone from Barnegat Light public works at the interconnect valve in Loveladies, near the tennis courts on Tidal Drive. Not only did Vosseller have to find the valve, which might be covered with sand, he also had to get to Tidal Drive, which he wasn't sure he could do given the flooding.

Back on the tractor, he drove up through Loveladies on the southbound lanes to avoid the sandy, swampy mess on the northbound side. Once there, they found the valve, turned the water on, and Vosseller headed back to the yard. He couldn't see a thing outside the tractor's meager headlights. Blackness enveloped the powerless night. He couldn't tell what kind of damage surrounded him.

When Vosseller got back to the yard he took a look at the tower level gauges. He couldn't believe it — they were dropping. *What the hell is going on here?* He had two guys on standby, so he sent them out to start checking for leaks. That's when he realized that there were houses with busted pipes.

The found a couple of houses with water spewing out and shut them off. But the tower level continued dropping. Vosseller got on the phone with the people in Barnegat Light and asked them to keep checking for leaks. The water had to be leaking from somewhere.

The crews got all the way up to tract 49 in Loveladies. It was a disaster area. Natural gas bubbled up through the wet sand. Houses had the bottoms blown right out of them with water spraying all over. Damage in Harvey Cedars looked minor compared to this. Crews stumbled across two luxury cars buried in the sand. *Why did anybody leave a car like that on the Island?* Vosseller wondered.

Earlier on, while Vosseller was losing water, Harvey Cedars Mayor Jonathan Oldham joined a crew patrolling in a military vehicle to assess the dunes. He wanted to see how much of the beach replenishment remained — if any.

At Mercer Avenue they noticed foam coming up over the top of the roadway. *Oh, this isn't good*, Oldham thought. *Were the dunes even there?* Even in the moonlight it was hard to tell what anything looked like. The vehicle made its way down the next street where water rushed around them. It caught Oldham by surprise. "I can't believe this!" he shouted.

At that point, the radio started to go off. 'I need to get rescued!" The same message, repeated over and over.

They made their way to Hudson Avenue. Conditions had gotten worse since Vosseller's last report. With the heavy truck on the pitched roadway, the team began to worry about the condition of the road.

"It was like a dam had broken and the water is going down the side of this truck and I'm afraid," Oldham recalled later. "I was afraid that the whole street end would be undermined and just drop. And we're sitting in this truck."

At the other end of the Island, in Holgate, the horn honked on the Hyundai in the Howards' driveway as water shorted out the circuits. At 9 p.m., the car floated down Jacqueline Avenue. It swung perpendicular to the house and headed toward the empty Mahoney residence next door. The car got caught on the front stoop, which had been built after the '62 Storm. It's not a wide stoop, but it's a strong one, and it held the Hyundai through the duration of the storm. Had it not, it likely would have crashed through a wall of the house.

After watching the car float away, the Howards watched water reach the circuit box of the house across the street, which belongs to Marilyn's sister and her husband. The circuit box exploded when the saltwater found the live current. Sparks rained over the deluge of water. Then the power went out and stayed out for the duration of the storm.

Despite the chaos outside, the Howards went to bed as Jacqueline Avenue's homes endured relentless pounding from the water and waves. They weren't watching when the surge ripped the entire front room off a small beach bungalow across the street to the east. All around them, breakaway walls were tearing apart. Whole sections of the lower decks on Hurley's Motel were lanced off, along with doors and in-wall air conditioners. Sand filled the empty voids where driveways and decks and stairs used to be.

One block north, a huge dark mass floated down Carolina Avenue. The Clarks watched it teeter its way up the street from their home on Bay Terrace. It seemed to take up the entire width of the street. It bounced off utility poles as it got closer. Then they recognized it. The little green house, number 6 Carolina, one of the original 1960s bungalows, floated toward the bay as though it were a houseboat — windows just above the water.

It barely missed slamming into the Clarks' home, but as it floated by it snagged something else — their Ford Edge SUV. Flooding had already destroyed the vehicle. The Clarks had watched as the water rose around the truck, shorting out the car's electronics. As it died, the Ford's headlights flashed and the horn blared as though signaling for help. The floating house couldn't clear the bay beach at the end of Carolina. It beached itself almost perfectly, facing the road, almost parallel to the street, looking as though it were built there decades ago. In what looked like its perfectly placed driveway sat the Clark's Ford.

Meanwhile, a half-mile south, Don and Clarice Kartan ventured outside. Darkness blanketed all of Holgate. The power out, they could only hear the debris crashing around; the piercing beams of their flashlights uncovered the scene in only small doses. They aimed their flashlights at the trailer. Don's toolbox floated despite the weight of the tools. Don needed the thousands of dollars of tools in the box to make a living, and they were in danger of being destroyed by saltwater. Water several feet deep rushed by at an incredible clip. Unlike his efforts to move debris earlier in the day, Don couldn't venture far in the dark without some assurance that he could get back safely. They pulled out a 150-foot heavy rope they bought before the storm. Clarice tied one end around Don. He walked down the stairs and, with the house acting as a breakwater, the water remained calm at the bottom. He slogged through waist-high water, but as he passed the mailbox and stepped into the street, the water suddenly became neck-high. The current was pulling everything west over West Avenue and down McKinley and around the row of new homes sitting south of the Kartan's trailer. He kept his bearings using the light from Clarice's flashlight. It was hard, but he kept his focus. Struggling to fight the current, he made his way across the street, at times standing on his tiptoes.

Using what little footing he had, he made his way toward his tools. All he had to do was grab the toolbox and get it back to the house. He made it to where the toolbox was hung up on a fence, but he saw right away that he was too late. He retrieved the toolbox, but saltwater had gotten in and the corrosion process could not be stopped.

Fighting the racing current and being tethered to the house made moving and swimming difficult. Pieces of wood with embedded nails and other debris cut at his legs. Then the rope around him came loose. He struggled to regain his footing and thought for a few fleeting moments he was not going to make it. Then his toes felt pavement and he pushed himself toward the house.

For the rest of the night the couple did not sleep. They continued their watch over their mobile home from across the street. As the night went on, the hope of saving it diminished by the hour. For the Kartans, Sandy had now taken too much.

Sandy's worst came under the cloak of darkness. Many recalled seeing the full moon at the time of landfall, but it was a lure. The false sense of a storm gone by was nothing more than a warning beacon for the devastation that would follow. Holgate and the wildlife refuge temporary became part of Little Egg Inlet. The surge wiped away dunes and destroyed homes up and down the Island, but the damage was far from over. Any energy the surge had not spent on the destruction of homes in Holgate continued on towards the mainland. With it, tons of debris — shrapnel — gained momentum in the open bay.

Video of Beach Haven appeared during a break on Monday Night Football.

CHAPTER NINE

Landing on the Lagoon

Wendy McCrann made a cup of tea and tried to relax as she watched the second high tide of the day rise in her Beach Haven West lagoon. The first one, thankfully, didn't make it to the top of the bulkhead out back. Out in the center of the lagoon, a large barge used for pile driving for docks and bulkheads, served as surrogate dock for four recreational boats. The barge belonged to family friend Tom Green, who has a marine construction company. Green would ordinarily keep the barge at his home on Cedar Bonnet Island, but he felt it would be safer in the McCrann's lagoon — a mile and half of open bay to the west. The brakes on the barge were set eight feet into the bottom of the lagoon. *So far so good*, Wendy thought.

It's not like the barge wasn't being tested. The anemometer on top of the garage was spinning faster than it had all day, showing gusts to near 80 mph. Parts of the McCrann's fencing had already blow down. Wendy's husband Mike busied himself taking measurements of the tide height off their bulkhead. Mike was once a commercial fisherman. He knew what he was looking for. Wendy could see him through the one window in the house that wasn't boarded up. He looked concerned. Mike came into the house to relay the news. The tide was rising five inches every half hour.

Wendy put her tea down and began moving their stuff higher in the house. Now there was a sense of urgency. Wendy and Mike went into overdrive. They even lifted the refrigerator and gas stove onto cinderblocks.

Wendy was tired, but there was no time to rest. Darkness was settling in. The cats were getting skittish, probably from the sudden drop in barometric pressure, or maybe the oncoming tide triggered some instinctual behavior.

Wendy didn't know. Outside, the lagoon was no longer a lagoon. The neighborhood looked like a lake as water came over the bulkheads and into the yards. There was still thirty feet between the water and the back doors of the house. Mike went outside to check on the tides again. When he returned, he told Wendy they had five minutes before the floors got wet.

They packed their bags and piled more family belongings higher in the living room. Wendy didn't even notice the water coming under the French doors behind her until she felt the cold bay water soaking her shoes and jeans.

With water now up to their knees, they remembered their car out front. "Move the car! Move the car!" Mike shouted. Only four months old, the sport utility still smelled new. It had all the bells and whistles. Wendy grabbed her backpack and dashed through the pelting rain to the driveway. She jumped in, struggling with her backpack to get behind the wheel, put it in reverse and backed onto the street.

But now what? Head to the cul-de-sac behind her or take a chance on Charles Boulevard, the one road that led out of the neighborhood? She drove toward Charles Boulevard, looking for a good place to park and still have the option to drive out.

The farther she drove, the deeper the water got. Wendy pressed on, accelerating slowly. The water rose halfway up the car's nineteen-inch wheels. Ahead, the road had turned into a navigable waterway. The tops of mailboxes, tall landscaping, and the houses functioned as navigational aids. Wendy started thinking about what it would be like to drown in a car.

She turned around and headed back to Patty Lane. Now the water flowed around the car and up and over the hood. It made its way up through the bottom of the engine and gaps in body panels, finding its way into critical wiring and motor parts, crippling them one by one. It was too much. The car died in the middle of the street. Warning chimes from the dashboard replaced the sound of the engine. Wendy listened to the frightening sound of waves hitting the outside of the car and the eerie sound of water *glugging* inside.

Wendy knew it doesn't take a lot of water to float a vehicle. If the wheels left the pavement, the car would be swept into the lagoon. She had to get out. She pushed the door but couldn't get it open. She pushed harder. The pressure of the water around the car was too much. She pushed again — even harder, and the door opened a crack. Water flowed in. She instinctively tried to close it again, but the water made it impossible. She stepped into the hip-high water and started walking, the water level lowering as she got closer to home.

On Cedar Run Dock Road a saliboat moored itself between a utility pole and a house.

A boat from a marina in Holgate travelled nine miles across the bay and salt marshes into the woods on Mayetta Landing Road, along with assorted debris.

"What are you doing?" Mike asked as Wendy walked up the driveway.

"I don't know where to go," Wendy said. "The car's stuck!"

The water kept coming into the house. They couldn't stay. Earlier that morning, a neighbor, John Popavich, said they could stay with him if they wanted to. Now they needed to. They corralled the cats into carriers, grabbed a few things and jumped into Mike's pickup truck, which was considerably higher than the SUV.

They drove past the abandoned vehicle and slowly made their way to Popavich's house, less than a mile away. When they got there, Mike drove up the driveway to within a couple of inches of the garage door. He offered to carry Wendy through the water to the steps to the house. She laughed. A nice gesture, and she thanked him for it, but her clothes were still soaked.

Popavich's house sat on ten-foot pilings, so the flooding was not a problem. They helped Popavich set up a generator and Wendy tried to recover from her experience. The wind shook the house. "Don't worry," Popavich said, assuring

The National Wildlife Refuge sign from Holgate settled in a large debris field alongside Newell Avenue in Beach Haven West (above), ten miles from where it stood. At left, a scene on Cedar Run Dock Road.

her the house was fine. "Don't worry?" she replied.

From the top-floor windows, Wendy looked down at her neighborhood. All she could see were the tops of mailboxes and houses. It no longer looked like home.

Down on Dock Road in West Creek, Debbie Murphy fought feelings of helplessness as she looked out a window on the second floor of a neighbor's house. There was an entire garage level below her, but the tides just kept getting higher and higher. She felt the water splashing against the garage ceiling less than a foot below her.

The house belonged to their neighbors, Mike and Jeannie Shima. Debbie and her husband Shawn had left their home and business, D&S Marina, at 5:30 a.m. It had taken on water by the time they woke up. Two feet of water had already covered Dock Road, the only way in or out. Dock Road snakes its way to Route 9, where Shawn had left his car — about two miles inland. The Shimas had offered their home and a ride. Mike Shima picked them up in an old 2½-ton "deuce" he bought off Craigslist only a few months earlier and drove to the house a half

In Tuckerton Beach, *I-Lean leans against a home (above); in the Manahawkin salt marshes of the Forsythe National Wildlife Refuge, a car is submerged (facing page); and boats and a shed nestle on the windward side of the storm at a house on Cedar Run Dock Road.*

mini-tsunami.

That final three-foot surge shook the house. The chandelier swayed. Then waves started slapping against the ceiling of the garage.

On Bonita Road in Barnegat Beach, a small lagoon neighborhood along Barnegat Bay in Ocean Township, Jill Belloff was trying to sleep. She had gone to bed around midnight, exhausted. Her body needed sleep, but her brain remained in crisis mode. She expected about two feet of flooding, something she and her husband Dennis could handle. But the uncertainty left them tossing and turning in bed.

At 2 a.m., sound of water woke her abruptly. It wasn't coming from outside; it was coming from downstairs. Jill jumped out of bed and hurried to the staircase. Water was splashing on the landing. It had come up through the floor and in through the doors, and now 18 inches flooded her entire first floor.

Everything she thought she had moved high enough was now floating, or tipping over. She ran back up the staircase and looked out the bedroom window toward Barnegat Light — normally her favorite view. But all she could see was more water coming straight at her. It sounded like a freight train. She watched wave after wave roll up the street. It seemed to be coming from every direction.

Jill and Dennis stayed upstairs for an hour and a half. Then they went down into the knee-deep water and walked outside. They looked around in disbelief. They expected this to be an Island event. But Sandy had come for them too.

Tuckerton Mayor Buck Evans signed the necessary paperwork declaring the

mile up the road. Debbie briefly entertained thoughts of a hurricane party.

All day they had watched the water rush in. They watched a neighbor's deck get ripped off and float away with two deck chairs still on top. It floated right between their houses. They watched a six-foot stockade fence get pulled from the ground and float away. Boats drifted by aimlessly. They watched as one boat, stored on land, floated — trailer and all — over a bulkhead and into the marshes. Debbie knew there was no getting out at this point. They were stuck for the duration.

Sandy's landfall Monday evening pushed another seven feet of water onto Dock Road. The Shimas and Murphys had watched the water level inch up all afternoon. The last push came in fast. And just when they thought it couldn't get worse, they looked east and saw a wall of water approaching. It looked like a town a disaster area a day before Sandy made landfall. Flooding had already begun in Tuckerton Beach and the early declaration allowed him to evacuate the area. Evans lives in Tuckerton Beach and he evacuated as well. He spent most of Monday at his office in the Tuckerton Seaport complex.

By Monday afternoon, water on the streets of Tuckerton Beach was almost as high as the fire hydrants. And it was supposed to be low tide. Residents who initially ignored the evacuation order needed to get out. The town sent fire trucks down South Green Street to pick them up.

Late in the afternoon the wind gusted up, snapping power lines off poles and exploding transformers in green and blue flashes. Evans ordered all first responders, police, firefighters and public works employees inside. He moved to Borough Hall. The Tuckerton Police Department facility on South Green Street had flooded, so police moved to Borough Hall as well.

Around 9 p.m. the winds subsided, and crews attempted another drive through Tuckerton Beach. They didn't get far. Green Street had flooded too severely. Floodwaters almost reached Main Street. Tuckerton Beach and Paradise Cove were cut off.

They tried getting through again at 2:30 a.m. Soon after they departed, the mayor got a call from the crew. A massive pile of about forty boats blocked South Green Street. It took four hours to slide and push the boats out of the way.

By that point it was dawn. Evans joined the crews for the first ride down South Green Street into Tuckerton Beach. They smelled gas immediately. It spewed from pumps at service stations that had been severed by the storm surge and debris. And they saw boats everywhere. Marina fences had broken, sending pleasure cruisers into yards and homes. Marinas looked like junkyards, boat after

Debris piled up on land and in the water in Tuckerton Beach.

boat piled up, facing all sorts of angles.

Most of the original homes stood no chance. Some sat several feet from their foundation. Others were partially collapsed. Some had fallen into the lagoons, where they sat half-submerged. Some who stayed said a seven-foot wave arrived with the last surge. Others said it was twelve feet. No matter, it did its damage.

Evans made his way to his own home. It was damaged, but he couldn't tell at the time if it could be saved. A few days later, a red sticker would be placed on the front declaring it condemned.

But there was no time to worry about his house. "Recovery mode starts today," the mayor told officials. Crews began clearing debris to allow emergency vehicles through. There were people still in their homes and they had to be tended to. They had to get the electric on and the natural gas off. Anyone not on official business had to leave. Tuckerton Beach was officially shut down.

A home in the bay, Cedar Run (above), and debris and a sailboat on Cedar Run Creek (facing page)..

Holgate.

NOVEMBER, 2012:

These Dark Days

CHAPTER TEN

Sea Change

The rasp of the old engine firing pierced the silence as the ex-military surplus truck traversed the sand piles that covered just about every inch of Holgate. On board were members of the Beach Haven Volunteer Fire Company, and they were getting their first look at what Sandy had left behind.

They figured they were the first because they saw no tire tracks. The truck forged through the mounds of wet sand and headed south past the Sea Spray Motel. They saw a sign on a store along the Boulevard still offering beach stuff and bike rentals. And they saw sand everywhere they looked. The way the tires struggled for traction, they knew it was deep.

Sandy had wiped out entire ground floors on the oceanfront homes to the east. The surge took away all the landscaping, dunes, and stone and brick paved driveways. Only clumps of wiring, fiberglass insulation, ductwork and pieces of pipe clung to the bottoms of the homes. From the truck, the rescuers could see the beach and the ocean all the way to the horizon — an impossible view prior to the storm. Now an open vista, they could see the jetties over the now-flat land. Beachfront homes sat on top of fully exposed piling. Sand fanned out over the northeast corner of the marshland between Webster Avenue and Rosemma Avenue. Beyond that, they could see the Mainland.

The truck, originally built for military service in 1967, struggled with the sand. A few times it got stuck. Two firefighters stood on the running boards of the cab, hanging onto the mirrors. Their job was to hop off to help push if it got mired in the wet sand.

Overhead, the thunder of National Guard helicopters occasionally blended with the rapping of the truck's diesel engine. Smaller news helicopters buzzed by as well, their gyro-stabilized cameras hanging from the tips of their noses, hunting for the first shots of Jersey Shore wreckage. Some of the men wondered if they would show up on the evening news. Their department pickup truck had already been shown forging through the flooded streets of Beach Haven during a news bulletin on Monday Night Football the night before. That brought a dash of pride to a chaotic night.

As they drove farther into Holgate the sights got grimmer. Houses lay pitched in sand, ripped from their foundations. Some had been gouged out by the ocean, their contents spilled out onto the sand. Fire company safety officer Stanley Markowski III could not believe he was looking at Holgate.

He saw cars on top of buildings, buildings flipped over on top of themselves, houses inside of houses, houses gone.

The first responders on the truck were all locals. They knew the streets. They knew the land. They cared about the people. They had risked their lives numerous times over the last 20 hours to make sure those who stayed made it through. Markoski took in the sights. He couldn't believe anyone rode the storm out here.

The smell of gas permeated the air. The first responders had already heard stories about a community in Breezy Point, N.Y., that burned down after gas lines were severed when homes were ripped from their piling. There was the fear that an errant spark or the operation of the truck or some other machinery would trigger an explosion. But they continued on.

At daybreak Eileen Bowker woke in a strange house. It wasn't a dream. They were at their neighbor's home. *At least I got in*

A wrack line of debris shows how high the water rose on the Causeway (above). At left and at top, Holgate.

some sleep, she thought. For a while she thought that wouldn't be possible. Not with all the commotion downstairs. The terrifying sound of glass breaking and water pouring into the garage, contents banging around and debris slamming against the bottom of the house. That and the thoughts spinning around in her head of what could be happening outside and whether her boys would be safe. Those must have been the "voices" that her friend had warned her about. Her two boys had slept soundly in the other room.

Eileen had prayed. As she prayed, she thought about her deceased father and uncles — hoping that they would somehow lend a spiritual hand in protecting their little deli and home. The prayer brought her just enough comfort and she finally drifted off to sleep.

Now awake, she walked over and looked out the window. The houses all seemed to be in the right places, but sand covered all of the roads and everyone's yard.

She and her boys quickly pulled themselves together and left to check on the deli and their home. Outside, absolute silence replaced the normal sounds of the shore. They heard no seagulls, no motorboats, no cars on the Boulevard, no sounds of neighbors walking on their stone yards. What yards? The sand unified the landscape. Many of the buildings may have stood in the right places, but they were damaged, some heavily.

They made it to the deli, considerably more easily than the trek they were forced to make a day earlier. Across the street, garage doors and breakaway walls had been ripped off oceanfront homes. The bed of a vintage Jeep truck poked out of a broken garage door. To the south, a sandy void replaced the municipal parking lot at the end of the Boulevard. Wiped out. The only hint a lot had been there came from the few remaining pieces of buckled, ribboned asphalt on its western edge.

The deli looked decent on the outside, but water had gotten inside. It looked like some gutting might be needed, but it could be salvaged. The yard was stripped clean. Almost nothing remained. But Eileen's father's decorative milk can somehow was still on the front porch right where she left it. And in the yard, the family's Celtic cross and Holy Mary statue survived. Eileen thought of the prayers she fell asleep to. She had a sense that her father

Holgate oceanfront.

and uncles heard her call for help. Upstairs, their home was intact. Home sweet home.

Eileen got right to work. She grabbed a mop and started removing the stagnant water from the deli. The boys went exploring, checking to see what kind of damage occurred in their neighborhood. They didn't get far. Near the Jolly Roger Motel, they heard a hissing sound and smelled the distinct scent of sulfur.

Duck Cove Marina at 32nd Street in Brant Beach.

Gas.

They rushed home, noticing along the way gas bubbling in the floodwaters in a couple more places. There was no way they could stay. The threat of explosion posed too much risk.

They headed out to their truck and, amazingly, it started right up. So they loaded it up and drove north, past the upside-down cars and houses that had floated off their foundations. But eventually, the sand and water proved too much for their small truck They headed back and waited for a rescue truck that could handle the terrain.

At least six inches of debris-laden sand covered everything. Commissioner Lattanzi stepped outside of his Haven Beach home to look around. *My God,*

Long Beach Boulevard in North Beach (above). Facing page: Three scenes from Holgate, and cinder blocks where boats were drydocked before the storm at a marina in Brant Beach.

I smell gas. Lattanzi wandered for a few moments to find the source. He picked up a distant hiss. As he got closer it started to sound like a jet. He followed it to a nearby house. The building had broken off of its foundation and the gas line feeding into the house was busted open. Working on instinct, he tried to improvise some sort of covering to cap it. No luck. He tried calling 911, but no one answered. *It is the morning after a natural disaster and every normal function of society and government is off kilter. No answer at dispatch. What has Sandy done to this island?*

A moment later, Lattanzi got a call back from Long Beach Township Police Lt. Paul Vereb. He called back from dispatch using Reverse 911. Lattanzi told him about the gas, and Vereb raced over to help him plug the line.

Lattanzi and Vereb cordoned off the area with yellow caution tape and returned to the Long Beach Township Municipal Complex in Brant Beach where Mayor Mancini, Police Chief Bradley, Captain Deely and a skeleton crew of officers had ridden out the storm.

As the center of Superstorm Sandy was winding down in Pennsylvania on Tuesday morning, Mancini brought the township's remaining first responders and police back from the Mainland. Then they began taking stock of the damage.

Mancini and Lattanzi jumped in the mayor's Jeep Wrangler and headed

it looks like a war zone, he thought. Sandy's surge had sucked up and spit out all types of debris from the massive to the mundane. Pieces of homes, personal photographs, cars and all sorts of other stuff tossed about with no regard to their importance. Covered in muddy sand, Beach Avenue had no delineation. The only hint that there was a street at all came from the street marker.

He looked down the street and saw the dunes had vanished. Garage doors were blown out by water and wind. Front doors and breakaway walls were in tatters.

toward Holgate. Driving down the Boulevard they could see that all of the towns had severe flooding. It seemed that every home and business saw some water. With each passing mile, the damage seemed to get worse. Once they passed Osborne Avenue, near the Beach Haven and Holgate border, things looked really bad.

Mancini couldn't help but think of the '62 Storm. He had been 12 years old then.

A home on Scott Drive had twisted off of its foundation and slammed into the house next-door, shearing off an entire section of it in the process. On Cohassett Road, another home was torn from its piling. On Inlet Avenue, a Cape Cod was decimated. The walls on the southern side had collapsed, and the entire structure had crumpled into a pile of wood and nails. Another house across the street stayed in one piece, but also was ripped from its piling. It, too, hit another home. On Joan Road,

Holgate (both pages).

a house sat partially in the road, its contents visible through the gaping holes debris had blasted through the walls. On the corner of Joan Road and Long Beach Boulevard, a ranch home was taken off of its foundation and sliced in half. The house right next door was reduced to just a shell.

Then there was the Long Beach Island Trailer Park. Waves had sent trailer homes careening through the park, metal meeting metal, ripping them open like sardine cans. The first nine rows of mobile homes on the east side of the

park were piled up like dominos. Most of the 142 mobile homes had been shifted and flooded. For the second time in a century, the trailer park was destroyed by a storm.

Continuing south, Mancini maneuvered his Jeep over large mounds of sand. They looked out to the east straight through homes to the ocean. Mancini was concerned. Without dunes, Holgate remained completely vulnerable if another storm were to hit. At high tide, water still flowed onto the Boulevard. Bulldozers

Holgate.

little sand remaining to support them.

Mancini remembered houses falling after the '62 Storm. He considered the vibration from the equipment and thought about the danger falling houses would pose to the workers. He quickly devised a temporary solution. The homes sitting precariously all had to be cross-braced.

Mancini and Lattanzi headed back to the township complex. Equipment was sent to Holgate and the mayor lined up some local builders to brace the homes.

The time had come for the leadership of all the Island's municipalities to develop a plan to get the Island back in working order. The Island needed to be reopened to residents and homeowners as soon as possible. But there was a lot that had to be done first.

Carl and Susan Clark woke up Tuesday morning and discovered their Holgate home on the corner of Carolina Avenue and Bay Terrace had been spared structural and flooding damage. The water came within inches of entering the house, but it never got in. The yard did suffer. The storm took their fence, and Carl's small trailer, which he used as a workshop, was swept across the street.

But when they took a walk to see what remained of Holgate, it didn't take long to realize just how lucky they were. The house that floated down Carolina Avenue remained perched on the empty bayfront lot just across the street. Their similarly transported Ford remained out front. Many of their neighbors' homes suffered severe damage, even destruction. Their neighborhood was not the same place it was a day earlier.

They walked toward the intersection of Carolina Avenue and Long Beach Boulevard. They have taken in this view thousands of times in all the years they lived here, but today it seemed unrecognizable. An old bulkhead had been exposed when dunes eroded directly east of Carolina Avenue. Water continued to flow around it and into the area that just the day before was the Boulevard. Piles of seaweed and dune fence formed in little bundles. In the center of the street, a light blue Volvo convertible sat buried in sand. Wind blew through its

had already been sent down to clear roads for rescues. Now they had to get the sand off the roads and onto the beach, where they would attempt to build a makeshift berm.

Looking around they realized that they had an even more pressing problem. Natural gas bubbled up through the water and sand. When Lattanzi opened the door to get out and investigate, the mayor pulled him back. The gas danger was too serious. The smell overwhelmed the senses. Holgate had far too many leaks for the two of them to deal with on their own. The mayor feared this might complicate sand removal operations. They needed the heavy equipment to clear the roads, but the gas made it dangerous.

Underneath many oceanfront homes, everything around the piling, including about 10 feet of filler, had been washed away. The homes stood with smashed windows.

They wandered around a few blocks, avoiding downed wiring, sinkholes, tons of debris and houses tossed about by the storm. Some homes had been pushed into the street. Some were pushed into other homes. It didn't take long for sensory overload to kick in. They headed back to their yard to check on the rose garden.

The rose garden, where Susan and her husband planted a new rose bush each season, appeared untouched. Some bushes would later die from the effects of the saltwater, but enough remained to give the Clarks hope for the future.

"Oh my god, there's a Cadillac in the back yard!" Marilyn Howard's gaze shifted to Jacqueline Avenue where, from her second-story window, just up the street from the Clarks, she could see the house across the street had lost its entire deck. Her sister's ground-level front door and windows had been blown away, and everything in their foyer was gone. "Look at Scott's car," Marilyn said as she looked up the street. The front third of neighbor Scott Darienzo's Buick convertible was sticking out of the garage. The car was a familiar sight on the block. Darienzo would stick his longboard in the back seat and cruise to his favorite surfing spots on summer afternoons. The garage doors were broken and the car had floated partially out.

Surf City

In the backyard, the Howard's shed, which housed their generator, had tumbled over to the Mahoneys' property next door, taking the outside shower with it. Most of their belongings were gone from the ground floor, including an exercise bike and a freezer. Their Lexus SUV managed to fight the tide and stay in the garage. But flooding caused enough damage to make it a total loss.

With no utilities and no water, Buzz and Marilyn Howard had to leave the Island. With both of their cars destroyed, they called for help. Township bulldozers took them from their home to the Boulevard, where they waited for

a National Guard vehicle to pick them up.

The Howards ended up at the Engleside. From there they were taken to a shelter at Southern Regional High School. They would later rent a car and drive to Rochester to stay with relatives.

Not long after the Howards arrived at the Engleside, Charlie Potter left to take a ride to Holgate in a four-wheel-drive vehicle. He and a friend made their way down the Boulevard after township bulldozers made the streets somewhat

A view from a Coast Guard helicopter shows Little Egg Harbor Bay enveloping Tuckerton Beach (above). To the south, in the distance, is Great Bay Boulevard, locally known as Seven Bridges Road, and the abandoned menhaden fish factory. Facing page: scenes of destruction in Holgate, across the bay from the view above, and a broken gas line in Surf City.

passable. Potter did not expect the damage to be so bad. His parents and grandparents were around for the '62 Storm. Memories of the stories they used to tell were on his mind as he drove. He recalled their photographs and old 8 mm footage of Holgate. *It looks exactly like it did back then*, Potter thought. *The houses are more modern, but it's basically the same destruction.*

They made it to Roosevelt Avenue. It was still flooded so they parked at the end of the street and waded through the filthy water to his house. It had flooded badly and would need to be gutted. He gathered his gun collection and some other belongings and headed back out.

Potter would spend the rest of the winter in a rental, located at the spot where the National Guard picked him up during his escape from Holgate. There he would spend a lot of time reconstructing the events of those couple days, from the walk to Beach Haven to the Sea Shell Motel's bar imploding around him and trapping him as seawater rushed in. They are stories he would share with friends. He survived, but he's not so willing to take the same chances the next time around.

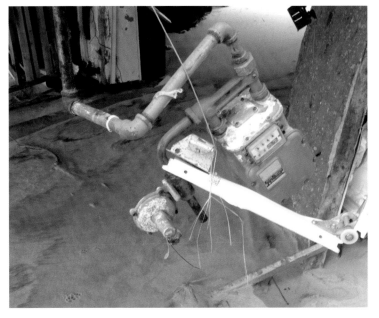

An aerial view of the Holgate Unit of the Edwin B. Forsythe National Wildlife Refuge (left), at the southern tip on Long Beach Island, shows overwash and temporary inlets carved across the Island, as the natural barrier beach absorbed the impact of Sandy.

Water got into virtually every structure in Ship Bottom. Farias Surf and Skate ended up with about four feet. At the Long Beach Island Grade School, the playground was ripped apart, and water flooded the basement, destroying electrical, phone, security and heating systems.

Pete Pianetti and Randy Townsend rode out the storm in Surf City. Pianetti was worried about his auto repair shop. Considering the amount of water he walked through to get out of Ship Bottom the day before, he didn't like the odds for his business. Tuesday morning he and Townsend suited up and made their way back to Pianetti's shop. Four feet of water had gotten in, but his tools survived. It was a setback for the new business owner, but he would reopen the shop by late winter.

Mayor Huelsenbeck and his entourage of Ship Bottom officials and first responders had come back from the Mainland in the early hours of the morning. By daylight they were assessing the damage. Some homes near the bay lost their entire first floors. Nearly every home suffered water

National Guard troops patrolled the beaches in humvees (above). At left, views of the destruction in Holgate, including an aerial of trailers repositioned like fallen dominoes by the storm.

He had gone to bed after a frantic attempt to stop the rising bay waters from getting into the empty first-floor apartment of the duplex he owns. He boarded and caulked the doors. It worked in the 1992 northeaster. It didn't work with Sandy. About six inches of water got in. When he felt the worst was over, he had gone to bed.

Wood owns Wood's Boat Service on 17th Street in Barnegat Light. Long Beach Island has been in his family's blood since the 1880s. He's an Island man. He maintains and services about forty sailboats a year from his back yard shop. He rode out the storm with friend Neal Kitson, a local commercial fisherman. His wife Cindy stayed on the Mainland with friends. On Tuesday morning, Wood and Kitson went out to the shop. When they opened the door, they saw the boats stored there were fine, even though the water made it as high as 11 inches — two inches higher than the '92 high water mark drawn on the wall.

Wood and Kitson then drove around town. Flooding had brought some headaches, but things looked relatively good. They got out of the truck on 4th Street and went up on a friend's deck to see the beach. Instead of the usual mile of sand, they saw nothing but water. Barnegat Light's massive beach remained completely submerged, and 15-foot waves continued to break in Barnegat Inlet.

They got back in the truck and drove south. At 29th Street they started seeing sand on the Boulevard. By the time they arrived at Coast Avenue in Loveladies, a water heater and toilet and other debris blocked the Boulevard. They could see six houses on that block alone that had been completely gutted — the lower levels ripped out and garages gone. *This is pretty serious*, Wood thought.

damage of some kind or another.

Once the initial shock subsided, the administration got to work. Word was spreading that some of the shore communities to the north of Long Beach Island got hit even harder and were starting to see a lot of fires. Firefighters went door-to-door inspecting homes and found and took care of eighteen gas leaks.

Dave Wood woke up in his Barnegat Light home knowing what to expect.

A convoy of National Guard humvees (above); at right the debris-strewn Boulevard looking north from Surf City into North Beach.

As they drove south through Harvey Cedars and into North Beach, the damage got worse. It became difficult to drive, even in four-wheel-drive. The sand was at least three feet deep and full of hidden debris. At the end of the divided highway, where North Beach became Surf City, the road opened up. No sand, no debris. They turned the truck around and headed back to Barnegat Light.

At dawn Tuesday morning, Debbie and Shawn Murphy noticed one of the boats from their business, D & S Marina, across West Creek Dock Road. The boat had floated half a mile west of the marina. Seeing that, the Murphys had no idea what to expect. A security camera Debbie accessed through her computer the afternoon before showed three feet of water on the marina property. Then the power went out, taking with it access to the camera.

The Coast Guard picked up Shawn and took him as close to Route 9 as they could get him by boat. From there, he hitchhiked to his truck. He then had to wait for the water to recede enough on Dock Road to be able to drive back to the Shima's house, where they had stayed the night, and pick up Debbie and drive to the marina. A few boats were scattered around the property, but most had drifted away. Only the cinderblocks the boats rested on remained. Sixty-three boats were missing. All of the docks floated off their piling and washed away. One boat landed on their well, putting a four-foot crack down the side. A 21-foot Silverton cabin cruiser sat atop one of the piling. As the water receded it must have dropped onto it from above, piercing the hull and entering the cabin. In the yard, the compressor, air conditioners, porches and the rest of the infrastructure were torn away or destroyed.

The full-service marina had taken years to build but just hours to destroy. The shop, office and the Murphys' household were all part of the same building. The shop, at ground level, had been entirely immersed in saltwater. All of the tools, machines, batteries and supplies were totaled. More than a foot of mud covered the floor. The high water line was two feet up the wall in Debbie's office, which is connected to the shop and sits slightly higher. The Murphy's home, which sits a little higher than the office, also had water damage. Incredibly, one of the boats had smashed through the window of their main living area.

The office was built in 2010 to the 100-year-flood standard. The Murphys' had invested in other improvements to the

marina that year — all up to code. The code hadn't counted on Sandy. Now the Murphys were looking at a long road to recovery. Still, while viewing the damage, they weren't calling this the end. They just had to pick up and start the recovery process. But first they had to find their customers' boats.

Mike and Wendy McCrann drove through Beach Haven West shortly after dawn, heading home to see how their house fared. The first thing they noticed was seaweed. It seemed to be everywhere. High water marks were visible on houses, mailbox posts, sheds — just about anything that was anchored to the ground. When they got to the house, they could see right away that it was a wreck. Everything was ruined. Water had made its way throughout.

Wendy stepped out into the back yard. The fence was completely down. Debris and more seaweed littered the yard. The barge and its four tethered boats remained in the lagoon. Somehow, it had managed to move about four feet closer to the house, even with brakes sunk eight feet deep. As powerful as the surge was, Wendy was surprised to see random survivors. She looked over at the Christmas tree they planted in the backyard in 2000. Underneath the tree a small yard ornament, a frog on a shovel, sat as though nothing had happened. Railroad ties that bordered the garden were damaged and some moved, but here was this little frog smiling away.

The surge up Charles Boulevard and Patty Drive swallowed her sport utility vehicle. The water went up 22 inches in the front of the house and 18 inches in the rear. It looked as though their home was one of the last homes hit. Only six houses to the west, everything seemed untouched. Wendy realized that if she had only parked to the west, she would still have a new car. At the time, the thought of heading toward a dead-end

seemed a sure way to lose it.

Later Tuesday, the McCranns shut off the gas to their home and the home next door. Few people had stayed in Beach Haven West, but some of those who did told stories about how the surge arrived. They said that it came in as a high-velocity, 6-foot wave, devouring everything in its way, with the homes at the end of Mill Creek Road taking the brunt of it.

Accessing the low-lying areas of Stafford Township quickly became Mayor John Spodofora's priority. Officials knew the vulnerability of Mallard Island, Mud City, Cedar Bonnet Island, Beach Haven West and Cedar Run Dock Road. He joined a crew Tuesday morning to take a look at the situation.

Spodofora saw boats on top of houses, cars in the salt marshes and lagoons and in the middle of the road. At times they had to move debris out of the

Carl and Susan Clark are evacuated from their home on Carolina Avenue in Holgate, along with a cat, by Long Beach Township police officer Patrick Mazzella on November 4. The police cruiser could not reach their home because of the sand. Facing page, top: A National Guard helicopter rises from the ballfield at the Ethel A. Jacobson School in Ship Bottom.

streets to get in and see if there were any people that needed to be rescued. He saw people who rode out the storm walking through the water carrying their most important possessions, wedding albums and things like that, clutching their arms, crying, walking through the water. He remembers it as being one of the most disturbing things he's ever seen.

Officials quickly took stock of the infrastructure. The water and sewer systems on Cedar Bonnet Island, Mallard Island and Mud City did not make it. Two water and sewer pump stations in Beach Haven West were destroyed. The Mill Creek Community Center did not survive.

Cedar Bonnet Island saw more than its share of damage, particularly on the south side where almost all houses were damaged or destroyed. Stafford's bay communities suffered immensely overall, in some areas sustaining damage even more extensive than the Island.

The Careys had no power, no gas and no running water. The three cars in the driveway of their Ship Bottom home were inoperable. Saltwater had destroyed the engines. One had a working battery and Patrick used that to charge the family's cell phones, their only source of information and communication.

The Carey's house is located close to the baseball field at the Ethel Jacobsen School. The field is often used as an emergency helicopter landing pad, so the sound of helicopters approaching didn't surprise them. As the sound grew louder and the helicopters got closer, the house began to vibrate. Dishes rattled in the cabinets. Skip ran outside. These were no medivac choppers. They were National Guard Blackhawk helicopters landing in the field. National Guard troops stepped out of the helicopter and began removing boxes of supplies and other cargo.

The Careys would get used to the thunder of the Blackhawk helicopters, but they had a tougher time dealing with the lack of utilities. Post-storm reality had begun to settle in. The Careys could not venture far on the street. The Ship Bottom police had set a curfew for everyone from 6 p.m. to 6 a.m. They advised people to stay home and not wander. The heavy law enforcement and

National Guard presence combined with the lack of utilities and isolation left Skip feeling trapped. He and the family could leave the Island at any time, but they would not be allowed back on. Still, it got tempting.

Two blocks away, Patrick's friend, Brandon, discovered that the Careys were still in town. His family had stayed as well. Risking being caught after curfew, he showed up Tuesday night with a basket of beer. The Careys also had a supply. Figuring some beer and wine would be good for everyone's sanity, the four of them spent the evening swapping storm stories.

At some point after 11 p.m., Skip quietly went upstairs and got out his bagpipes. He walked out the front door and stood in the middle of the street. *Forget you, Sandy!* he thought as he began playing. First "Minstrel Boy." Then "Kelly."

Meanwhile, Brandon had gone out back to relieve himself of some beer. When Skip blew the first notes into the dead silent night air, Brandon jumped nearly as high as the roof. He ran inside yelling, "What the hell…" Patrick smirked. "That's just my dad playing Sandy away."

Holgate (facing page and above). The Long Beach Island Trailer Park has a National Guard presence.

CHAPTER ELEVEN

Badlands

Sandy was now a slowing swirl of clouds and rain far west of Upper Darby, Pa., and Jim Mahoney was thinking about his home in Holgate. So many questions. Was the house still there? Was it damaged? What kind of damage? What does it all look like? The last photographs he saw where those Charlie Potter had posted on Facebook. They showed the dune break Potter passed on Monday. Mahoney recognized it as Jacqueline Avenue, his street.

Mahoney surfed through Internet sites and social media to try to find out more. What he found wasn't pretty. Entire neighborhoods destroyed. Quaint homes along Raritan Bay and multi-million-dollar mansions in Mantoloking reduced to rubble. An oil tanker beached in Staten Island. One photograph showed Seaside Heights' iconic boardwalk in splinters, the Sea Star roller coaster sitting just beyond the surf line.

He found posts from Beach Haven on Facebook showing water up to the windows of Chicken or the Egg and creeping up the steps to Fantasy Island's arcade. A resident staying above Island Books in Beach Haven posted photographs and video of Murphy's Market, How to Live, Uncle Will's Pancake House and Kapler's Pharmacy, all inundated by several feet of water. Videos showed first responders riding wave runners through even higher floodwaters. He found images of Brant Beach, taken from the air, showing streets covered with brownish muddy sand. Pictures taken over Spray Beach showed boats scattered in the streets.

Then he found news footage taken over the Island that showed southern Beach Haven. But just when his house was going to come into view, the footage stopped.

Hours later a neighbor who had also been looking for photographs of Jacqueline Avenue posted an image taken from aerial news footage that showed the street from the northwest. The image was low-resolution, making it difficult to see details. Water still flooded the west side of the street. Sand covered the yards and the road, although a bulldozer cleared part of the eastern half. His neighbor's home to the west blocked the view of his house, but at least he now knew it hadn't floated into the street.

Mahoney and his friends and neighbors put together a Facebook page called Holgate Update. An hour after the first post, Holgate Update's fan base had jumped from nine to 200, and people posted constantly.

One photograph showed the row of oceanfront homes across from Jacqueline Avenue and Joan Road. The storm had leveled the dunes, leaving a stark, flat beach. The ocean could be seen through piling now fully exposed under the homes. Long Beach Boulevard was covered with giant chunks of concrete and sand. Mahoney had walked past those homes only a few days earlier and countless times before that. More posts showing more destroyed homes followed. The Holgate Update Facebook page grew grimmer.

During the week, Long Beach Township police officer Patrick Mazzella and

Only the roof of this home is visible in the debris floating in a tidal creek along Jennings Road in Beach Haven West. The house was lifted off its pilings and carried during the surge from Cedar Run Dock Road, three miles away. Facing page: Holgate.

A cabin cruiser travelled the tides attached to its floating dock into the woods along the marshlands of Cedar Run; the Long Beach Island Trailer Park in Holgate; a sad Saab washed off the shoulder of Cedar Run Dock Road; a view of oceanfront homes along the sand-covered Boulevard in Holgate.

other officers took photographs of homes owned by friends and neighbors. Sometimes the imagess revealed a home had been spared. Other times, the officers faced the difficult task of sending a photograph of a destroyed home to its owner. On Friday, Mazzella, who had grown up in Holgate, sent Mahoney a text message with a photograph. It was a straight-on, street-level shot, and it showed an intact house that appeared to be sitting firmly on its foundation.

Now he couldn't wait to get there. He looked through the journal his late father kept. His father wrote a lot about the '62 Storm. Their house floated off the foundation then. He wrote about the town finally letting people back to see their damaged homes. Mahoney realized that it might take a while before they let people back.

Seventy-five year old Gerard Schultz couldn't stay at his daughter's home in South Brunswick any longer. He made the right decision to go there with his wife. They couldn't stay in Tuckerton Beach. But now that the storm was over, he needed to go back. Leaving his wife and daughter behind, he got in his car and headed south.

When he got to South Green Street, a barrier blocked the road at the Marshall Avenue intersection. No one was allowed in Tuckerton Beach. Schultz grabbed his Tuckerton Fire Police jacket and badge from the backseat and walked to the roadblock. Sgt. Chris Andersen agreed to take Schultz along as he patrolled the area.

As they drove down Parker Road, Schultz saw that some of the houses that used to sit along the bay had disappeared. Many of the area's ground-level bungalows sat in ruin. Gas mains hissed as they drove by. "I can't believe what I am seeing," he told Andersen.

They headed over to Anchor Road so Schultz could take a look at his home. Schultz was one of the lucky ones. Some shingles and siding blew off and the enclosures underneath the house had water damage, but the living area survived. The house was raised on 10-foot piling about a decade earlier. Looking around, Schultz could tell from the water marks that the storm surge was about five feet.

Schultz stayed at the Inn at Sea Oaks until Tuckerton Beach reopened, and he helped man the roadblock at Marshall Avenue. No National Guard. No State Police. Only the Fire Police ran that roadblock. Schultz had to constantly turn away people he knew. Everyone had an excuse to go to their home. Some had pets. Some had medicines. But Schultz couldn't let them through.

Schultz also heard stories from those who rode out the storm. One man who lived right along the bayfront had to retreat to the second floor of his house. He said he saw the bay build up about a half hour after the wind shifted to the southeast. Even up on the second floor, waves splashed against the windows. Another man thought he was going to die. For 5½ hours he heard waves and wind pounding his house. He was afraid of drowning or electrocution if he fled, but each moment he stayed he feared broken gas lines would cause an explosion.

Many residents said they saw the storm surge coming. Most said it came from the east-southeast, near the inlet, and it looked like a 12-foot wall of water with a three-foot wave on top of it. Others said they saw 10-foot waves breaking in the bay.

Nine days later, Schultz finally moved back into his house. A different neighborhood greeted him. Officials had tagged houses with red tags and green tags. Red tags meant the home was uninhabitable. Green tags meant the house was habitable. Not many people stayed around. Of the thirty-five homes on his street, only a third were occupied. An uneasy quiet blanketed all of Tuckerton Beach. The constant fear of looters kept everyone on their toes.

Ten miles north, in Beach Haven West, Wendy and Mike McCrann went to work immediately, gutting the house, filing claims and getting the ball rolling on the recovery effort. Although it suffered immense flooding damage, they weren't interested in a new house. Wendy is a part-time public adjuster, so making inroads through the insurance maze came as second nature.

After a few days, Stafford Township had cleared enough of the roads for the McCranns to take a ride around the neighborhood. There were not very many people around. Some of the people they talked to who live along Mill Creek Road told them the surge came in as a six-foot wave that destroyed everything in its way. The homes at the end of Mill Creek Road took the brunt of it. Driving down there the McCranns saw massive devastation. They took a drive down near Harbor Village and looked at the marshland. It was a landfill of junk, unhinged docks, boats and all sorts of debris — some of which made its way all the way from Holgate.

In the coming weeks, the contents of everyone's home would end up in giant piles on the street. For the McCranns and others staying in Beach Haven West, every day was emotionally draining. Residents lived in a daze. A few weeks after

Boats in the wrong place in Holgate (above). At right, the support wires for a utility pole tell the tale of the storm with salt hay driven by waves and wind all the way to the top.

the storm Wendy was driving their old beat-up sport utility vehicle. She drove along, freezing, without realizing she had the hatch up the entire ride.

On the Friday after the storm, Jill Belloff looked around her Barnegat Beach neighborhood. Boats and personal watercraft ended up everywhere. A dank, dark mix of sand, silt and lagoon muck covered everything. It smelled terrible. It took until Wednesday afternoon for the water to recede enough to start shoveling some of the muck up into piles in the yard. The township had promised to bring a backhoe in to remove the piles.

Through the week, residents met at the municipal building. Gift cards were circulated. They had been donated for people in need. People in need. Belloff never expected to be someone in need. Her maiden name is Svelling, and she comes from a long line of fishermen. Her father's family left Norway for a new life in Barnegat Light in 1929. Her father, Captain George Svelling, was born in Barnegat Light and

worked as a fisherman all his life. He taught her to work hard for what you earn, and to stand firm and be stubborn when it comes to things you believe in.

Belloff needed that strength now. Like everyone in her neighborhood, Sandy stole what they worked so hard for. The neighbors held hands. They helped each other cry and helped each other laugh, and they promised to help each other rebuild.

Ray Fisk and Leslee Ganss live at the end of Cedar Run Dock Road, directly across Little Egg Harbor Bay from the Long Beach Township municipal

Views along Cedar Run Dock Road, where the storm surge barrelled up Little Egg Harbor Bay toward the Causeway, leaving boats and wreckage in its wake, including the first floor of Antoinetta's restaurant. Facing page, left: Harvey Cedars Marina.

complex and Bayview Park. Three miles from Route 9, they are surrounded by the bay and the salt marsh of the Edwin B. Forsythe National Wildlife Refuge. Their home is located in one of the few genuinely isolated spots along the shore. With a full view of Long Beach Island south of the causeway bridges to Atlantic City, they documented on Facebook the days after Sandy from this desolate vantage point on the edge of the bay:

October 30 — Tuesday morning:

Tried to go in chest waders to our house, but tide was still too deep and wind was knocking me over in the open marsh. I'll try again later. From two miles away I saw our house still standing, but I'm sure everything at ground level washed away. If I can make it back and get in I plan to camp there and assess. The tide was 5' above the road at the upland end of Dock Road so I'm sure we took a big hit. From Mayetta Landing Road at the bridge —2½ miles from our house — I walked a half mile east and most ground level structures were destroyed. Lots of boats, a few cars, scattered in debris.

[Later that day] I made it ... and am camped out here for the night at least. Three miles out into the bay, darkness all around. So strange not to see the string of lights that is (was) Long Beach Island across the water. There are only two solid lights, a handful of strobes flashing from the Causeway to Beach Haven, then Atlantic City is aglow to the south. Manahawkin is dark. The hike down Dock Road was disturbing but not a surprise: Boats everywhere — on the road, tipped into the marsh, slammed into homes. Cars abandoned. Everything at ground level was hit with the force of waves. My neighbor's little shotgun-shack of a home (which survived '62 and '92) is gone. Vanished. Only a few pilings and his mailbox remain. His well continues to bubble up water, oddly. I called him. It was like telling a friend that a child or parent had died. We were incredibly lucky. Everything above the first floor on pilings is just as we left it. But below: An almost clean slate. Walls, stairs, shelves, all the utilities from the electric service, the furnace, the well pump, my tools, Leslee's horse tack, shoes, off-season clothes, and boxes of old family items are gone. There is a debris field of heavier metal objects. All the boats and kayaks, tied securely I thought, are lost. ... I am humbled and grateful.

Gas leaks are everywhere.... Our meter was hissing out gas, a neighbor's pipe was

completely snapped off, spewing away. I found a wrench in the sand and shut them all off. For the little house that washed away, it's just gas bubbling out of the wet marsh; I couldn't find a shut-off.

October 31 — Wednesday morning:

I woke up in my own bed (in my clothes, in a sleeping bag) and for a brief moment — with dawn beckoning over the bay — thought everything was normal. Until I saw eelgrass at the top of a utility pole. From wind or waves? Some storm.

There are a few local cowboys who work around the restrictions and rules. At 6 a.m. a guy was at the boat ramp. The Island is closed so he took his boat to his mother's flooded North Beach Haven house, and trudged through debris to retrieve her medications.

Leslee made it to the outpost — and found Halloween lights and one Christmas decoration in the debris. Two holidays covered!

October 31 — Wednesday night:

I could get used to looking out my windows at night and seeing in the moonlight a primitive and completely dark island, Causeway, and Manahawkin... Not that I wish for any delay in restoring power, but it is wild and beautiful. Feels like I've been transported to another age.

November 1 - Thursday:

The State Police let me through a new blockade tonight, and again the road is dark, desolate, and still debris-strewn. I felt the need for a walk around this eerie, flood-ravaged world. The Causeway remains pitch black as is the entire length of Long Beach Island and all of Manahawkin that I can see. I can't get over what an extraordinary experience it is to be alone here at night at the end of this road, miles into the bay and marsh, with no light but the moon reflecting off the water. The water that tonight seems so gentle and calm but destroyed so much. The price that has been paid for this observation is extreme, so I think I owe it to everyone to say it. What a privilege.

November 2:

I observed the incremental re-lighting of Long Beach Island and the Mainland. [Until then the only lights were the distant buildings of Atlantic City to the far

Boats and abandoned cars littered Southern Ocean County's roadways, here on Cedar Run Dock Road. Utility wires snagged the tuna tower on the boat at left.

south.] My candles are getting a little competition: There are now streetlights in a section of Brant Beach north of St Francis Center!

November 3:

Causeway bridge lights are on!

November 4:

Six days later, I'm still trying to wrap my head around the biblical proportions of this storm tide. I thought I understood the potential: 1935, 1944, 1962, hurricanes Belle and Gloria, Halloween '91, and December '92.... None of these storm tides exceeded a

Heavy equipment was required to carve paths through sand-clogged streets in North Beach — and throughout the Island. Moving the wet sand one front-end-loader scoop at a time was a time-consuming process.

certain height; '44, '62, and '92 were all within inches of each other as the record. But Sandy's tide was a magnitude or two greater. It's the difference between human history and geological history, I suppose.

[Holgate was still dark, but:] *Final LBI lighting report from the Dock Road outpost: The Island is illuminated from the Causeway to Beach Haven. This side of Manahawkin and Beach Haven West and our sad road remain dark.*

There were fascinating and scary forensics from the electrician who disassembled our service panel: *He could tell from the burned wires that we had power to the house as the ground floor walls ripped away with the breaker box and electric meter. As they went under the waves, everything shorted out, sparking and crackling into the pitch black of the storm, while the gas line seperated, spraying gas into the night. For that experience alone I am glad I did not stay.*

CHAPTER TWELVE

These Dark Days

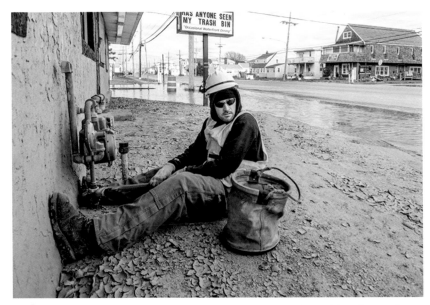

Workers scrambled to repair natural gas lines (above), and National Guard troops in humvees patrolled the beach while the Island was off-limits to residents (facing page).

As National Guard Blackhawk helicopters patrolled over Manahawkin, a line of cars built up in the eastbound lane of Route 72. The cars were driven by homeowners anxious to see what remained of their homes. One by one, they arrived at "Checkpoint Marsha", the gateway set up by authorities at the intersection of Marsha Drive and Route 72. Long Beach Township and Stafford Township police officers stood guard, rifles in hand. One by one, they told the drivers the same thing: No.

Anyone crossing the causeway bridges had to pass through "Checkpoint Marsha". Those heading to the southern end of the Island had to pass through a checkpoint in front of the Long Beach Township Municipal Complex. Those heading to Holgate had to also pass through a checkpoint at the Holgate-Beach Haven border. Those heading north had a checkpoint at North Beach. Officials also set a curfew from 6 p.m. to 6 a.m. Local law enforcement and the National Guard hoped the checkpoints and curfews would curtail looting, but some were feeling hassled by what they felt was undeclared marshal law.

You could either stay on the Island if you were already there, or you could leave. If you left, you couldn't get back until officials re-opened the Island. No one knew how long that would be. Only those carrying all-access cards or whose names were on access lists could get through checkpoints, and only those providing essential services had cards or were on the lists.

The first concern was gas. Mains had broken all over the Island. Gas-related fires had already destroyed entire communities in Brick Township and Breezy Point, N.Y. By Wednesday officials shut down the pipeline that serves the entire Island. Water had already been shut off and electricity had been down since the height of the storm. Those who stayed now had no utilities.

At night, the National Guard kept watch on land and sea using night vision and heat-sensing surveillance equipment. The Coast Guard and State Marine Police patrolled the bay. The Louisiana State Police helped Island police patrol the streets. Long Beach Island had become a military zone.

Holgate residents Don and Clarice Kartan couldn't sleep much. Sometimes they woke to flashbacks of the storm. Other times they were kept awake by fear of looters. They welcomed the sight of the National Guard for security, but their presence only reminded them of the condition of their neighborhood. It no longer felt like home. Normal routines like biking for coffee or heading down to the wooden jetty to surf had vanished. Holgate sat in shambles. Everything surrounding the Kartans was depressing and unrecognizable.

The home they stayed in was fine, but without utilities it was hard to function. Across the street, their home at Farreny's RV Park sat in ruins. Water flooded all of the battery compartments underneath, rendering it a total loss. The only good that came out of it now was the propane. Clarice cooked meals in the busted trailer and brought the food across the street to eat with Don.

Their only connection to the outside world came through their cell phones.

Many streets and parts of the Boulevard were impassable until heavy equipment could clear beach sand overwash deeper than snowdrifts.

Fortunately, the Kartans had parked their two cars at high elevation and they survived. They couldn't drive anywhere because the roads were blocked with sand. But they used the cars to charge their cell phones.

There weren't many people left in Holgate. Some of those who rode out the storm, including the Bowkers a block away, had been rescued the day after landfall. The neighborhood was vulnerable to looters coming over from the Mainland in small boats. One day, Don came across two men in a boat who claimed to be out of gas. Amazingly, the boat's engine started right up and they zipped across the bay when the conversation turned to the National Guard.

The Kartans were getting concerned about the health effects of the gas leaks. They didn't know what was in the water they had been walking through, or in the sand.

On Thursday morning, they loaded a few belongings and their pets into Don's Jeep Wrangler. It still ran well and the tank had enough gas to get them off the Island. Clarice maneuvered the Jeep through slippery muck and over sand piles. They hit dry pavement near the border of Holgate and Beach Haven and kept going, off the Island and on to northern New Jersey to stay with Don's parents. The Kartans would eventually return to the Island. They would replace the trailer home with a new, slightly larger one. And they would consider themselves pretty fortunate.

Only a few blocks north, on Bay Terrace and Carolina Avenues, the Clarks

At "Checkpoint Marsha" on Route 72, a sign answers the question, "When can residents return?"

The beach scene in November featured bulldozers, humvees, and camo wear.

made it through the first week. They endured the silence that accompanies a world without electricity, phones and the luxuries of modern life. With each passing day, the sight of their neighborhood became harder to bear. By Sunday they had had enough. They called in a rescue request. A Long Beach Township police officer responded. The Clarks grabbed as much as they could carry plus their three cats in carriers. Carl sat in the front and Susan got in the back with the cats and the luggage. Driving out of Holgate, Susan felt a bit like a hostage behind the thick bulletproof window between the front and rear passenger sections. When they arrived at the Shell Station on Route 72, the Clarks' daughter, Kimberley Hawes, was waiting to pick them up. Susan pulled the door handle and quickly discovered she could not get out of the vehicle on her own. The officer had to walk around to open the door. Their daughter, in a serious tone, asked, "Mother, what are you doing in THAT backseat?"

One of the cat carriers held the feral kitten that came in during the storm. The Clarks took her with them to Pennsylvania. An animal rescue organization member would later adopt her and name her Survivor.

Governor Christie met with first responders and the press in Harvey Cedars at the High Point Volunteer Fire Co. on November 7, ten days after the storm.

Angela Andersen and her family made it through the storm just fine, riding it out in their neighbor's house in North Beach Haven. When they returned home, they discovered that water did enter the first floor of their home. It rose just high enough to cause damage, but the house could be fixed.

Andersen's bigger concern was her father's oceanfront house on 80th Street in Beach Haven Crest. When she approached the house she could see immediately that the entire ground floor had been washed out. The ocean swept clear through and into the neighbor's yard. Anything she had not brought upstairs before the storm had washed away. But the house was still standing. After losing two homes to the sea, her father made sure to provide extra support when this house was built 1969. He used 35-foot piling when the township only required 25 foot. Andersen stared at the piling. It looked as though at least 25 feet had been exposed.

Angela's husband Jim spent the days after the storm cleaning debris and retrieving boats from sedge islands. While out there he saw that decks, docks, refrigerators and other household debris had clogged up the bay. So much sand washed into it as well. He worried about the navigability of the waterways.

In Harvey Cedars, Jason Marti, Scott Oswald, CJ Alyanakian and Chris Oldham take a break from securing utilities on oceanfront homes on Wednesday afternoon.

Living on the Island while it was closed to the public, you could either make the best of it or let the worst of it eat you up. Some chose to tough it out with old friends while making new ones. Jack Bushko had no intention of leaving.

He made it through Sandy alone. During the storm, he felt the fear. Staying on the top floor of the apartment above Island Surf & Sail in Brant Beach, he managed to make it through the night with just a flashlight, headlamp and video camera by his side. All night he heard the wind and debris banging off things inside and outside the shop. When morning came, he dusted himself off and moved on.

Provisions were delivered to first responders working around the clock at fire houses, such as here in Surf City, and functioning municipal buildings.

least the steaks would have. At night, he would gather wood for a fire and sit in front of the flames in a rocking chair, feeling much like an Islander from the 19th century..

As a local watersports instructor, Bushko already knew most of the locals and police officers. The National Guard quickly got to know him, and everyone let him be. He kept an eye on the store and the neighborhood, and law enforcement checked on him to make sure everything was going well.

Bushko managed his situation well. He would explain later that it was all about staying in a survivalist mindset. "Some people can, some people can't," he said. "You just pull real deep from your gut when you have to. In hindsight I wouldn't stay again, but it's something to say that I did."

Skip Carey didn't attract the attention of the police when he played the bagpipes in the road in Ship Bottom after curfew. But when he started getting cabin fever after a few days and went for a drive, the police stopped him and told him to go home.

The Careys spent their days cleaning out the garage, checking in with family on

Bushko walked down to 68th Street. His neighbors had told him to help himself to their houses if he needed shelter or food. He decided to take them up on that. After making the rounds, he had accumulated a pretty good assortment of food and a pretty nice beer collection. He found a propane tank Sandy had deposited and a grill that washed up. Every day he would grill the neighbors' steaks and drink their beer. It would have gone bad otherwise. At

their cell phones, and using the Internet. None of their three family cars made it through the flood. Like Bushko, they called their neighbors for permission to raid their refrigerators. They had to cook everything on the gas grill in the back yard. They even made spaghetti on the grill one night. Occasionally family friend Joe Rulli, who owns the Joey's Pizza chain, stopped by with a pizza or a tray of wraps. He made runs from his Stafford location, bringing food to law

Scenes from the recovery: Alabama Power Co. crews help restore electric service to the area; navigating sand-clogged streets on the Island; the Long Beach Island Trailer Park park in Holgate.

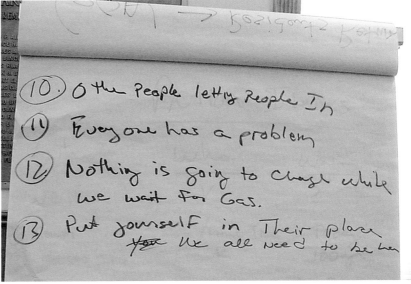

10.) 0 the People letting People In

11) Everyone has a problem

12) Nothing is going to change while we wait for Gas.

13) Put yourself in Their place. You We all need to be here

Checking for gas leaks; a destroyed kitchen at Joey's Pizza and Pasta in Beach Haven Crest; and some flipboard thoughts for first responders and others working on the closed Island.

...and was on side streets and over the Boulevard, everywhere except where it was needed — on the beach. Emergency, man-made dunes were quickly sculpted by the Army Corps of Engineers, here in Harvey Cedars.

Retailers like the Hand Store in Beach Haven returned to find that merchandise had floated, sunk, or just absorbed the tide. The Dutchman's restaurant on Cedar Bonnett Island lost part of its familiar sign, but re-opened quickly to serve first responders and repair crews restoring services on the Island.

With the Island closed, Manahawkin's "Checkpoint Marsha" on the west side of the Causeway turned away all but critical traffic. Governor Christie met with first responders in Harvey Cedars ten days after the storm. A white board outlined a daily recovery action plan.

enforcement, troops at checkpoints and people at firehouses. When he dropped food off at the Careys, Skip and Trisha invited neighbors over.

Still, no bathroom facilities and no showers made life a struggle. As the cold November air settled in, the lack of heat added to the issues. But the Careys handled it. For Skip, one of the toughest parts didn't come until homeowners were allowed back on the Island. He found it difficult watching people see their damaged homes for the first time, especially the elderly. He thought about how hard it must be to have to start over that late in life.

Joe Lattanzi and his wife led a convoy of three vehicles off the Island on Wednesday. As a Long Beach Township commissioner, Lattanzi had a pass to get back on the Island, but everyone else knew the trip would be one-way. One of the evacuees was an 80-year-old woman who rode out the storm alone. When news arrived that the caravan had to leave early in the day to avoid high tide, she expressed concern about having time to do her hair before the trip.

After dropping everyone off, Lattanzi headed west to Medford. He had a second mission. Mayor Mancini had asked Lattanzi to get some earth moving equipment. National Weather Service was talking about a possible northeaster approaching. With only a small berm built using sand removed from the Boulevard and side streets, plans immediately went into high gear to get more bulldozers and front end loaders to build stronger, higher berms.

Lattanzi had a friend in Medford who owns six bulldozers and offered to rent them to the township. He ordered them and his friend assured him that they would arrive the following day. True to his word, the bulldozers arrived in Stafford on Thursday, but they couldn't get past "Checkpoint Marsha". The driver wasn't on the access list. When Lattanzi showed up, he was furious. "What the hell do you think they're here for?" he shouted. Police let them through. The berm was built before the storm arrived and the Island avoided any further dune breaches.

The isolation and lack of utilities would wear on everyone who stayed, including the first responders. Beach Haven firefighter Ric Anastasi knew he needed to stay focused on doing the job. As long as he was busy he wouldn't think about his severely damaged home, wouldn't think about the damaged and destroyed homes of people he cares about. But the slow start of recovery provided plenty of time to think. Every day felt like a repeat of the day before. *Nothing gets any better, nothing gets any worse — just exactly the same, every day."* Anastasi and other members of Beach Haven Volunteer Fire Company No. 1 whose homes had been damaged stayed at the Engleside Inn in the days and weeks after the storm.

In Long Beach Township, Harvey Cedars, Ship Bottom, Surf City and Barnegat Light many of the first responders lived at their respective fire stations or municipal buildings. They slept on couches, floors, tabletops, the back of vans and trucks in between shifts. Many had homes that were damaged or destroyed.

The National Guard housed its troops in the Long Beach Township municipal complex. The men slept on the floor in the meeting room. The women slept on the floor of the mayor's office.

Only if a firehouse had a generator was the luxury of a hot shower possible. In Beach Haven, firefighters used their mobile decontamination unit as a shower. That was outdoors, in November. People lived in close, uncomfortable quarters for weeks. It was a recipe for a meltdown. But it didn't happen. Politics and drama did not exist.

Many who stayed on the Island had nowhere to cook,

National Guard, humvees, and bulldozers on Long Beach Island's beaches (above). Facing page: North Beach sand at Lagoon Drive S. and the Boulevard; the Marsha Drive checkpoint in Manahawkin had the look of a base camp with trailers and facilities.

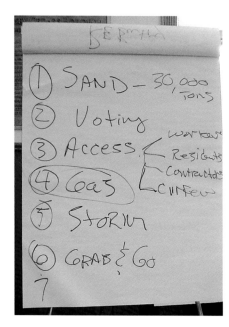

Facing page: Restaurant owners were allowed limited entry into Beach Haven on November 4 to begin cleaning out their businesses, including Barry's Do Me a Flavor, the Chicken or the Egg and the Bagel Hut. Above, mountains of sand in Holgate, a loggerhead turtle is a storm victim, debris and sand at the Sea Shell in Beach Haven. At right, a flip chart shows the enormous problems to be dealt with in the recovery.

A water-filled drawer at Joey's Pizza & Pasta in Beach Haven Crest (left); an oceanfront home repositioned, above.

and for many the Island was cold and lonely. The firehouses filled that void. As the days passed, more and more of the community visited their local firehouses for meals and companionship.

In Surf City, the Surf City Volunteer Fire Company and EMS building became a haven. At first, only about fifty people stopped in, mainly to charge their cell phones and swap stories. Word spread fast, and soon 200 people stopped by the firehouse for breakfast, lunch and dinner every day. Donations from all over the state kept everything going. At first, Judy Hartney, a 21-year EMS veteran, drove the ambulance over to the Mainland to pick up donations. She would return with an ambulance full of milk, eggs, food and supplies. At one point, a tractor-trailer arrived with donations from Delran. The truck had so much to unload, EMS workers had to move apparatus out of one bay to fit it all in. Volunteers sorted all of the donations and set up the ambulance bay like a food pantry. Residents from all over the Island could come in and eat a hot meal and take whatever they needed — from cleaning supplies to nonperishable food.

Locals not only used the shelters, they also volunteered their time to help out. Someone was always cooking at the Surf City firehouse. An electric stove was donated so meals could be cooked despite the lack of natural gas. When Scott Russo, a part-owner of ScoJo's restaurant in Surf City, got on the Island to check on his business, he cooked some meals at the firehouse.

The Barnegat Light Volunteer Fire Company served as many as seventy meals daily. As food thawed in people's homes, they brought it over to the firehouse to be cooked. Volunteer Ron Roloson helped

There were many priorities after the storm, but clearing the streets of sand was at the top of the list.

out at the High Point Volunteer Fire Company in Harvey Cedars. He doesn't even live in Harvey Cedars. He was staying with a friend. But he stopped in and washed dishes and cooked a little. He even manned a garbage truck and helped pick up debris around the borough.

Steve DiPietro scanned the property of his small restaurant on 34th Street in Beach Haven Terrace. Four walls stood tall and windows were intact, the roof untouched. The giant sign remained high atop the two rusted poles, the California Grill sun logo proudly displayed.

Within hours, the Grill's insides were outside. It was full-sanitizing scrub down time. Wet sheetrock, damaged equipment and a few waterlogged electrical outlets were tossed in the dumpster. Food in the freezer and walk-in refrigerator out back went to a local shelter and firehouse.

DiPietro was determined to get the California Grill operating quickly. Someone had to feed all the workers.

His other restaurants, the Dockside Diner in Spray Beach, the Bluewater Café in Haven Beach, and Stefano's in North Beach Haven all needed work as well. Stefanos and the Dockside Diner flooded badly. The diner was actually punctured by a wayward Sunfish sailboat. But DiPietro wanted to get the California Grill opened first.

New Jersey Natural Gas crews were restoring gas on the Island one section at a time. When they made it to Beach Haven Terrace on November 16, the California Grill was ready. With most of the restaurants in the area closed, it quickly became the central hub for cuisine, coffee and conversation.

The Army Corps of Engineers builds an emergency dune line in front of oceanfront homes in Harvey Cedars (above). At right, the Sea Shell in Beach Haven and sand removal in Harvey Cedars.

Sandy knocked many Island businesses out of commission, but local business owners still helped out the community in any way possible.

Halina Breitling of 4-Bee's Polish American Deli & General Store in Surf City cooked for first responders and others working on the Island. The Coast Guard was so grateful they presented her with a flag that she proudly displays in her store.

Brothers Richard and David Schmid emptied out the refrigerator at their Cedar Bonnet Island restaurant, the Dutchman's Brauhaus. They donated all of the food to the shelter at Southern Regional High School and to the High Point and Surf City fire stations on the Island. Cedar Bonnet Island's gas lines were not part of the Island shut-down. Once the gas company tested and certified their lines and once electricity was restored on Saturday, November 3, the Schmids began making food for local shelters, first responders and law enforcement. By Monday, David Schmid could be seen running from checkpoint to checkpoint in his Chevy Trailblazer, passing out hot food. The brothers also opened Dutchman's doors to utility workers and Cedar Bonnet Island residents in need of a hot meal.

Business owners were allowed on the Island on Saturday, November 3, to survey damage and remove perishable food. Residents from all towns except Holgate and North Beach could check their property's condition on Monday, November 5, but they couldn't stay.

Cars had already begun to line up at "Checkpoint Marsha" on Sunday night. By morning, the line stretched for miles out Route 72 and up along the Parkway. At first, everyone had to show proof of residency and each car would get a colored placard that indicated which Island town they had access to. It didn't take long to see that wasn't going to work. Eventually, they just opened the checkpoint.

The process of gutting homes had to wait, but residents and business owners immediately began piling everything that had gotten wet at their curbs. By the time the 3 p.m. cutoff arrived, piles of debris lined the streets from Loveladies to Beach Haven.

CHAPTER THIRTEEN

Reunion

The wait was over. A dozen days had passed since Sandy hit, but it felt like months. Long Beach Township had allowed residents to check on their homes previously, but Holgate and North Beach weren't included. Too dangerous, officials said. Now those areas were being opened to residents for their first "grab and go" session. Just enough time to get in, check their homes and get out.

Jim Mahoney left Upper Darby, Pa., at 5 a.m. His wife, Sue, and friends Jill Chudyk and Charlie Nolan joined him. They made their way down Route 72, through the Pine Barrens. The autumn weather was clear and crisp. Trips to Long Beach Island usually created an atmosphere of joviality in the car, but this time Mahoney felt anxious.

By the time he arrived in Stafford, traffic had already backed up a mile at "Checkpoint Marsha". Police and National Guard vehicles blocked the median and the shoulders of the road. Men with machine guns and rifles stood guard. The line moved slowly, but at least things were moving. Finally, Mahoney pulled up to the officer checking for documents. He presented his documentation proving that he owned a home on the Island and drove on.

Normally Mahoney's stress would go down as he drove over the Causeway. Now his anxiety actually increased. Approaching the Ship Bottom circle, empty lots and darkened windows replaced the normal hubbub of businesses operating along the road. The always-busy Wawa was vacant, badly damaged by flooding.

Along Long Beach Boulevard, plywood covered the windows of closed businesses. Trailers surrounded Ship Bottom Borough Hall. Store after store appeared lifeless. Mahoney couldn't tell which ones might reopen and which would simply go away.

Continuing south, past Long Beach Township's municipal complex, signs warned of curfew times and explained where FEMA offices were located. Massive piles of trash lined the Boulevard. Yards looked bare, missing tapestries and sections of fence. The roads still held a dusting of sand. As they drove through Beach Haven, the town never looked so quiet.

Construction on the Boulevard prevented a normal entry into Holgate. Mahoney had to detour to West Avenue and up Merivale Avenue, where an early model Ford Taurus sat lifeless on the street behind the roller hockey rink. The car was missing fascia on both sides and seaweed covered the exposed seats.

Traffic slowed around the re-entry point to the Boulevard just north of a checkpoint that had been set up near the Sea Spray Motel. Long Beach Township police officers mingled with men in fatigues from the National Guard. A military Humvee sat on the corner of Osborne Avenue and Long Beach Boulevard. Mahoney could feel the tension rise. He had seen the photographs, and he had a bad feeling about what was waiting for them.

When Long Beach Island was first re-opened to residents for a "grab and go" day, traffic was backed up for miles on Route 72 in Stafford Township (above); additional checkpoints validated residency on the Island (right). Homeowners were likely to find family memories scattered amidst the debris (facing page).

He cleared the second checkpoint and continued south. Everywhere he looked he saw huge mounds of sand. He drove past Webster Avenue, and the first of the severely damaged oceanfront homes came into view. He had seen plenty of heavily damaged oceanfront homes on the ride down the Island, but seeing these shocked him. The news photographs didn't prepare him for this. The homes, which once sat high on a dune with raised and landscaped driveways, appeared much smaller on exposed piling. Wires, insulation and plumbing hung from the bottom of the homes. Mahoney's wife and friends took pictures from the car windows. It was an amazing sight, seeing beneath the houses all the way to where waves were breaking on the shore.

Holgate was humming with activity. Bulldozers moved sand from yards and streets onto the makeshift berms. National Guard Humvees mixed with family sedans and pickup trucks. Uniformed troops walked the streets. Hundreds of Holgate residents circled the area, looking for a place to park so they could get a first look at their homes.

As he approached southern Holgate, the damage got worse. The sea had

In Brant Beach, at 82nd Street, an oceanfront home crashed into another house (right); a Southern Regional yearbook floated old high school sentiments into the debris fields (above).

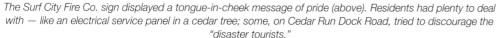
The Surf City Fire Co. sign displayed a tongue-in-cheek message of pride (above). Residents had plenty to deal with — like an electrical service panel in a cedar tree; some, on Cedar Run Dock Road, tried to discourage the "disaster tourists."

moved houses. Homes had been destroyed. Homes Mahoney had driven by countless times lay in pieces. The damage made the entire neighborhood seem foreign. He followed the trail of destruction to Jacqueline Avenue, where Hurley's Motel sat stripped of its usual adornments. The bottom floor looked like a shell. Its deck railings sliced off, staircases gone and sand everywhere.

Mahoney turned the corner. The street was alive with friends and neighbors, yet the houses appeared deserted. The damage took his breath away. Familiar faces crowded the streets. Four feet of sand clogged his driveway, so Mahoney parked his car across the street. He saw the Hyundai Sonata perched on his front stoop. He walked around and looked at the rest of the house. The structure looked sound. The windows and doors appeared intact. Some of the downspouts had been torn down and the electric meter had been pulled from the wall. It must have been whipping around on the service cable because it damaged the siding and a nearby window frame. Mahoney thought the house looked pretty good, all things considered.

In Beach Haven West, as throughout the region, curb-appeal took on a new meaning as residents emptied their storm-ruined contents.

He hoped the inside fared as well, but looking around the yard and the neighborhood, he knew it was a long shot. He and Sue walked to the front door. It wouldn't open. He tried a couple more times then gave up and walked around to the back door. That wouldn't open either. He went back to the front door and threw his weight into it. The door swung open. The first floor had flooded. A water line on the wall two feet high showed how much. Everything from bookshelves to furniture had been washed around.

Everyone stood there, stunned. They

The storm punched through this home in Holgate, leaving dune fence and debris inside (above). It was Halloween, and this decoration in the debris seems to have encountered more than just a "boo."

Loveladies (facing page and left): On the oceanfront, rooms and garages at ground-level felt the wrath of Sandy first.

A garage with a view (above). Facing page: Sandy leaves her calling card in a once-cozy hearthside space in Loveladies, while salt hay and bay mud coat a living space in Cedar Run, and family pictures are scattered by the tide.

expected water damage, but seeing what it had done shocked them. Mahoney looked around. The old house held a lot of personal items and memories. Now they were all spread out on the floor. Treasured books were now trash. Furniture was destroyed. Every room on the first floor told the same story. The porch sat in a similar state of disarray. The contents of the dining room were spread all over the house. Toward the back, the floor had fallen in. Small sections of plywood had floated away, leaving gaping holes in the floor.

Mahoney didn't know where to begin. *What the hell do I do now?* He only had a few hours before he was supposed to leave, but he was overwhelmed. He needed to get out. He grabbed his camera, left Susan and his friends, and walked around the block. Susan knew how much the house meant to him. It had been a part of his life since he was a kid. She understood why he had to walk away.

Mahoney stepped out onto Jacqueline Avenue. The sight of all of his

neighbors and friends was bittersweet. It felt a little like a block reunion, but there was no party. Everyone looked to be in a state of disbelief. They smiled as they greeted one another, but their expressions held an underlying look of sadness. There were tears and hugs.

Mahoney greeted his neighbors as he walked. Everyone had a story. Everyone

The parking lot at the Acme in Beach Haven Park (facing page) and other locations like the bayside lot at Bay Village in Beach Haven became transfer stations for the storm debris that mushroomed on Island streets. Specially equipped double-trailer trucks with what many residents dubbed "the claw" were a common sight at the end of 2012.

Boats at docks, boats in storage, boats on trailers all ended up scattered throughout the Island and Mainland. These watercraft were deposited on Carroll Ave. in Tuckerton Beach.

shared the damage assessment. It just felt better to talk about it. Mahoney walked past the front room of a house that had been washed four yards west, crushed and buried in sand. He walked past a home with two destroyed cars in the garage — an S-Class Mercedes and a vintage Corvette. As he turned the corner of Joan Road, a white Chevy Tahoe police vehicle from Louisiana drove by.

He walked toward the beach. Drew Hoinash, who owns a house on Joan Road, was running from yard to yard with a T-wrench, helping neighbors shut their water valves. Farther up the street he came across a house sitting partially in the road. Its western eve had hit the house next door. One wall of the wayward house had been ripped open, revealing clothes still hanging neatly in a closet. A Tiffany lamp sat on a table upstairs. Mahoney knew the house. It belonged to Charlie Smith, one of the original residents on the block. Across the street, waves had broken another home completely in half and sent it into a neighbor's house.

Mahoney walked up to the Boulevard. An endless procession of cars passed by. Every car seemed to have at

An oil painting of a boat floated and settled on this waterlogged sofa in a mud-filled summer home.

Storm-ruined debris was pulled out of homes that could be saved in Beach Haven West (below, and facing page), but in many cases the structures were beyond saving.

least one passenger taking photographs or video. He crossed the street and walked around the massive sand piles that were being laid out for the construction of a berm. Looking out at the ocean brought instant relief. With his back to the destruction, the beach looked the same as it always looked. Jetties still bordered Beach Number 3 to the north and south. Waves gently rolled up the flat, wet sand and mixed with shells. Mahoney thought for a moment about just staying there and letting the images of devastation drift from his mind. But he had to get back.

Mahoney crossed over the Boulevard to see Carolina Avenue. He walked past a huge sand pile with a blue Volvo buried at the top. A bulldozer put it there to get it out of the road. He walked toward the bay, past an empty lot, and stopped. Short piling stuck up out of the sand. The McDermotts' house sat on those piling before the storm. Mahoney flashed back to memories of playing cards there as a kid. He looked toward the bay. The house now sat in the Green Acres lot at the end of the road. The deck was wrapped around a utility pole a few feet up the road.

Mahoney walked for an hour. He took a photograph of a

woman sitting on her property, staring into space with a puzzled look. He felt like he knew what she was feeling. He saw a lot of people who faced a more difficult recovery than he did. The walk revealed things he never expected.

Mahoney found himself back at the west end of Jacqueline Avenue. Time to face the music. He could see a pile of house contents had already formed in his yard. He jumped up on the front stoop, dodged the Hyundai, and went into the house. Susan and his friends Jill and Charlie were rummaging through the house, taking anything soggy and tossing it. Mahoney looked at them and smiled. They had taken the first steps for him. He felt some of the anxiety melt away. The long road to recovery had begun.

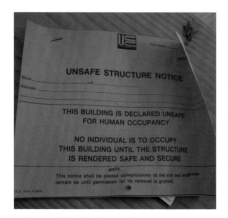

Orange "Do Not Occupy" notices were as common as stranded boats and broken break-away ground level structures. Insurance claim numbers were even more prolific.

A Holgate home settled on top of a pile of beach sand — and was inserted into another house.

Holgate (above left) and at the Long Beach Island Trailer Park (facing page). Siding at this home in Tuckerton Beach and on a yardstick shows the height of the tide (left); above, a kitchen on Cedar Run Dock Road.

Coming Back to Life

The summer of 2013 might be remembered as the summer that was "Stronger Than the Storm," a slogan aggressively marketed in a New Jersey tourism campaign across the tri-state area. It's more than a catchy jingle — the Jersey Shore *is* stronger than the storm. With so much revenue at stake, towns along the Jersey Shore raced to be back by summer. Local and state economies depended on it.

And in many ways the Jersey Shore did make it back. Restaurants, nightclubs, shops, amusement parks and miniature golf courses opened. In most cases, you could still enjoy the beaches — still surf and swim and do all of the things you have always loved to do at the shore.

And the campaign did what it was supposed to do: It got people back. The casual observer might not even notice anything had changed. That, of course, is testament to the will and dedication of a great many people who made it happen.

But while the businesses that were able to open got a marketing boost from the state, thousands of home and business owners were still struggling with insurance claims, FEMA applications and rebuilding well into the summer. Some grappled with the possibility that they might not be able to come back at all. Some did not have insurance. Some did not get enough money. Some lost everything with little or no hope of any happy ending. In between the open signs and lit up homes sat darkened storefronts, newly vacant residential lots, gutted homes awaiting restoration and houses that continued to lie in ruin. Not everything was stronger than the storm.

Just ask Dennis and Jill Belloff. They got right to work preparing insurance claims on their flooded and damaged house in Barnegat Beach. The Belloffs always paid their flood insurance. They were sure they were covered. But the township ultimately determined the house needed to be demolished and rebuilt from scratch, something a disputed $60,000 settlement check from the insurance company wasn't going to cover.

Now, as the Belloffs appeal the settlement, they rent in Forked River and continue to pay the mortgage and insurance on a house that was condemned. They are far from alone. Similar stories exist behind virtually every home that sits vacant — and there are plenty from Mystic Islands to Pebble Beach and all along the Island.

The shore would not have made it as far back as it has without the legion of volunteers who came out to help despite their own Sandy-related problems and personal losses. Countless people donated food and money, many spent days gutting homes and clearing debris, and others organized large volunteer cleanup and recovery events.

Trucks lined up to dump removed sand in Surf City, where it was deposited on the beach (above). In the months after the storm, many fundraisers took place (left); in addition to funding Sandy relief efforts, they provided the community with healing and carthatic social gatherings.

Harvey Cedars (above) and other towns on Long Beach Island quickly began using bulldozers to push the beach into artificial dunes to protect homes from winter storms. But much sand was where it shouldn't be — Island streets and the Boulevard — and it needed to be moved (facing page). At right, above, an overwash of sand in the Holgate Unit of the Edwin B. Forsythe National Wildlife Refuge shows the natural migration of a barrier beach westward, in contrast to the developed portion of Long Beach Island to the north.

Stafford Teachers and Residents Together (START), a group run by Joe Mangino and Mike Dunlea, had 2,000 volunteers who logged more than 13,000 hours cleaning more than 700 homes in Beach Haven West. The Alliance for a Living Ocean organized beach cleanups and continued research and educational programs exploring Sandy's traumatic impact on the local environment. AmeriCorps, AmeriCares, and numerous religious and church-based organizations helped people gut their homes and remove debris. Various chapters of the Fraternal Order of Police donated money and supplies from all parts of the country. Mutual aid fire and EMS companies helped run relief centers and organized food and supply donations. The Red Cross brought food and a hot cup of coffee to those fixing or gutting homes on cold winter days.

Southern Regional High School sophomore Jimmy Ward wanted to do something unique. He posted a video on YouTube showing him running through the devastation on the Island in a black t-shirt proclaiming the word "HOPE." In less than a day, 9,000 people viewed the video. People told him it brought them to tears. By February, it had more than 30,000 views in more than 100 countries. Ward was asked in the spring to produce a sequel for Long Beach Island's "LBI is Alive" campaign.

Sandy brought out the very best of people in the very worst conditions. Fr. Steven Kluge of St. Francis of Assisi in Brant Beach saw volunteering bring new hope and new faith in the people in his parish. "There is a beautiful prayer that says our love for God becomes perfect when it reaches our neighbor. And that's really shown throughout this Island. People's love for God on this Island is being shown by how we are treating our neighbors," he said.

Jetty founders Jeremy DeFilippis and Corey Higgins have made community outreach a cornerstone of the local surf and skate apparel brand. With experience running surfing contests and raising money for social causes, Jetty was able to step in immediately. On the Wednesday after Sandy struck, DeFilippis and Higgins set out to design a t-shirt to raise funds. They released the "Unite & Rebuild" shirt that night and had 2,500 shirt orders in two days. The shirts were a staple of their grassroots fundraising efforts and by spring they had sold

Scenes from a recovery, clockwise from left: Flooded and closed banks brought in trailers for temporary operations with ATMs; local restauranteurs, despite their own difficult circumstances, organized a huge community Thanksgiving dinner; surf apparel company Jetty raised several hundred thousand dollars for storm relief; an appropriate page from a book found in the debris fields; mountains of sand were screened at the end of the Island in Holgate; and stranded boat removal was a challenge throughout southern Ocean County.

more than 20,000.

Local journalist and surfing magazine writer Jon Coen used his contacts to help Jetty partner up with Waves4Water, a non-profit international disaster relief organization founded by professional surfer Jon Rose. Rose taught them the Waves4Water blueprint. Rose also provided Jetty with the funding and resources needed to begin organizing relief efforts through Waves4Water LBI Outreach.

Jetty organized groups to help raise money, gut storm-ravaged homes and clean beaches. It worked with community groups like START, the Jersey Shore Chapter of The Surfrider Foundation, ALO and others. They worked with Rick McDonough, Coen and his brother Brian, Randy Townsend, Dan Volardi, Chris Huch, Brian Farias, Amy Williams, Melanie and Eric Magaziner, Tom and Elizabeth Beaty, David Calderella and Joe Mangino to organize thousands of volunteers who cleaned more than 1,000 houses. Between November and July, Jetty raised and distributed almost $300,000.

Researchers from the Coastal Research Center at Richard Stockton College, including director and founder Dr. Stewart Farrell and geospatial analyst and Holgate resident Dan Barone, surveyed the beaches immediately after Sandy. For decades the center has regularly measured changes to the beach due to natural physical processes and episodic changes from storms. They also analyzed how engineered structures, such as groins, jetties, seawalls and beach replenishment can alter beach-dune systems. After Sandy, the researchers collected beach profile data from 105 monitoring sites on the New Jersey coastline. Their data backed up what many felt already — that beach replenishment worked.

"The biggest takeaway of all was that the Army Corps design really worked," Farrell said. "It actually stopped the waves before they got to the development to cause damage. That would be Harvey Cedars, Surf City and Brant Beach, and of course Barnegat Light borough which had a naturally very wide beach due to the change in the inlet jetty."

In Holgate, where dune damage was extensive, some dunes survived. Farrell attributed that to beaches being wider in those spots, but he also noted that the dunes that survived also had been taken care of obsessively well by the owners of the beachfront homes behind them. Adding dune fencing and vegetation helped considerably.

For many returning homeowners, a first look at the wreckage was a question of where to begin (left), but for Island municipalities the place to begin was with sand removal (right). Emotional moments of unity occurred with community events like the Beach Haven holiday tree lighting and caroling at the Long Beach Island Historical Museum (facing page), and with winter clothing offers, like the one at the community Thanksgiving dinner at Southern Regional Middle School (facing, left).

For months after Sandy, local municipalities and residents pressured holdout oceanfront homeowners to sign the easements needed for new beach replenishment projects. Governor Christie and local mayors publicly expressed frustration at the holdouts, and more signed each week. Meanwhile, the Army Corps raced to complete scheduled replenishment projects and repair beaches where replenishment had already taken place. As summer started, many were startled to find beach closings as barges pumped in sand in Harvey Cedars,

Surf City and Brant Beach. They had a greater appreciation for the protection these disruptions brought. Some even lent their voices in the planning and implementation of future projects. They accepted more responsibility for the beaches they have always loved.

Nearly nine months have passed since Sandy. We placed an added significance to the little events that mark the passing of Island time: the opening of the

A berm is constructed, creating an artificial dune line in Harvey Cedars (above) as a buffer against winter storms. (Facing page): Sand removed from streets is screened for debris before being deposited in Holgate.

Chicken or the Egg, the turning on of the traffic lights, lifeguards going on duty. We anxiously waited on the Friday before Memorial Day to see if cars would back up on Route 72. They did. And in so many ways we have showed that we have indeed survived Sandy.

But we aren't quite the same. Sandy taught us some lessons that can be quantified — we learned we need to build our houses higher and our beaches wider, that we need to do something about flood insurance, and so on. But look closer than that. Look into the eyes of the people who stayed in their homes when Sandy visited. You'll see the legacy runs a little deeper.

This was the storm that would never happen. We were all pretty sure of that. But now when you talk about Sandy, you see quick glances at the ground, pauses in the conversation, doubt. It would never happen, but it will happen again. That's what you're seeing in those eyes. A fear of what could be, but also a new respect, not just for the storm, but also the forecasting and evacuation calls that precede it.

But when this does happen again — and we get knocked down and beaten up by yet another storm that turns left instead of right — we know this: We will get back up and start putting things back together. That part has not changed since 1962, or 1944. Life on Long Beach Island and the Mainland will go on. On the winds of catastrophe, Sandy delivered the same message to a new generation — rebuild, restore, and come back stronger and wiser every time you do.

Some things were not stronger than the storm, and restore/rebuild rhetoric aside, it was the end of a Causeway icon — the Shack.

Bibliography

Books

Buchholz, Margaret T., Savadove, Larry. (1993) *Great Storms of the Jersey Shore*. Harvey Cedars, New Jersey: Down the Shore Publishing.

Lloyd, John B. (1990) *Six Miles at Sea: A Pictoral History of Long Beach Island, N.J.* Harvey Cedars, New Jersey: Down the Shore Publishing.

Pilkey, Orrin H., Nordstrom, Karl F., Neal, William J., et al. (1986) *Living with the New Jersey Shore*. Durham, North Carolina: Duke University Press.

Publications

The Ocean County Sun. "The Great March Storm, 1962."

The SandPaper. "Special Edition: Beyond Sandy." Spring, 2013.

State of New Jersey. New Jersey State Police. State of New Jersey Office of Emergency Management. (October 26 - 30, 2012) *Situation Report(s) #1-3, #3.3, #4-7, #8.2, #9, #9.2, #10, #10.1, #10.3, #10.4, #10.5, and #11* by New Jersey State Emergency Operations Center. Retrieved April 20, 2013 from http://www.co.hunterdon.nj.us/911/oem/Sandy2012/

United States. National Oceanic and Atmospheric Administration. National Hurricane Center. (2013, February) *Tropical Cyclone Report: Hurricane Sandy (AL182012) 22-29 October 2012* by E.S. Blake, T.B. Kimberlain, R.J. Berg, J.P. Cangialosi and J. L. Beven II. Retrieved March 27, 2013 from the National Hurricane Center Web Site: http://www.nhc.noaa.gov/data/tcr/AL182012_Sandy.pdf

Internet Sources & Articles

Abrams, E. (2012, October 22). *Sandy, The Gale of '78 and Warmth*. www.AccuWeather.com [Web log post]. Retrieved April 21, 2013, from http://www.accuweather.com/en/weather-blogs/abrams/sandy-the-gale-of-78-and-warmth/545226

Associated Press (2012, October 24). Hurricane Sandy slams into Jamaica en route to Cuba. *CTV News*. Retrieved from http://news.google.com.

Bates, T. (2013, January 15). Sandy 'waterway debris removal zones' set in N.J.. *The Asbury Park Press* (www.app.com). Retrieved June 20, 2013 from http://blogs.app.com/enviroguy/2013/01/15/sandy-waterway-debris-removal-zones-set-in-n-j/

Bella, T. (2012, December 21). What I Found at My Jersey Shore Home in the Aftermath of Sandy. *The Atlantic*. Retrieved from http://www.theatlantic.com/national/archive/2012/12/what-i-found-at-my-jersey-shore-home-in-the-aftermath-of-sandy/266546/

Castillo, M., Almasy, S. (2012, October 26). Sandy kills 11 in Cuba, then batters Bahamas.

Among the more benign items in Sandy's debris fields were books, including these sentimental children's favorites, read long ago.

CNN. Retrieved from http://www.cnn.com/2012/10/25/world/americas/tropical-weather-sandy

Coen, J. (2013, July 10). Shore Protection and Sandbars in One: A Straw of Hope regarding Beachfill? [Web Log Post]. *The SandPaper*. Retrieved from http://thesandpaper.villagesoup.com/p/shore-protection-and-sandbars-in-one-a-straw-of-hope-regarding-beachfill/1027341?cid=80384

Coyne, K. (2007, July 8). A Keeper: Surfer's Island Trailer Park. *The New York Times*. Retrieved from http://www.nytimes.com/2007/07/08/nyregion/nyregionspecial2/08colnj.html?_r=1&

Ekwurzel, B. (2013, April 17). Grappling with Sea Level Rise Before and After Hurricane

Sandy: Film "Shored Up" Leaves No Sand Grain Unturned. Union of Concerned Scientists. Retrieved on June 10, 2013 from http://blog.ucsusa.org/grappling-with-sea-level-rise-before-and-after-hurricane-sandy-film-shored-up-leaves-no-sand-grain-unturned

Englund, E. (2012, November 18). Beach Haven Relocates Operations to Emergency Operations Center. *The SandPaper*. Retrieved from http://thesandpaper.villagesoup.com/p/beach-haven-relocates-borough-operations-to-emergency-operations-center/926779?cid=107719

Essinger, K. (2012, October 29). Some Residents Fear Storm; Others Don't. *The SandPaper*. Retrieved from http://thesandpaper.villagesoup.com/p/some-residents-fear-storm-others-dont/916973#.UX21PBwoKzY

_____. (2012, October 30). Ship Bottom Family Ditched Island Last Minute. *The SandPaper*. Retrieved from http://thesandpaper.villagesoup.com/p/ship-bottom-family-ditches-island-last-minute/917439#.UaC95BwoKzY

_____. (2012, November 13). Island Opens Permanently, Except in Holgate. *The SandPaper*. Retrieved on June 21, 2013 from http://thesandpaper.villagesoup.com/p/island-opens-permanently-except-in-holgate/924471#.UX28WhwoKzY

Governor Christie (2012, October 27). Governor Christie Press Briefing in Monmouth County On Hurricane Sandy. Retrieved June 10, 2013 from http://www.youtube.com/watch?v=rMuksUXwZYM&NR=1&feature=endscreen

Hayes, M. (2012, October 27). Christie cancels Romney campaign trip, will be in state when hurricane hits. www.northjersey.com. Retrieved June 10, 2013 from http://blog.northjersey.com/thepoliticalstate/5402/christie-cancels-romney-campaign-trip-will-be-in-state-when-hurricane-hits/

Homenuk, J. (2012, October 22). Hype meter rising on potential weekend storm: What's the deal? www.nymetroweather.com [Web log post]. Retrieved April 21, 2013, from http://www.nymetroweather.com/2012/10/22/hype-meter-rising-on-potential-weekend-storm-whats-the-deal/

Johnson, P. (2012, October 31). Sandy Devastates Sections of Tuckerton, Little Egg Harbor. *The SandPaper*. Retrieved from http://thesandpaper.villagesoup.com/p/sandy-devastates-sections-of-tuckerton-little-egg-harbor/918144#.UaC-mRwoKzY

Kaszas,-Hoch, J. (2012, November 3). Natural Gas System Shut Down in Wake of Storm. *The SandPaper*. Retrieved from http://thesandpaper.villagesoup.com/p/natural-gas-system-for-lbi-shut-down-in-wake-of-storm/919519?cid=1218943

Lassonde, V., Englund, E., Kaszas-Hoch, J., Scandale, M. (2012, November 2). Long Beach Island Damage Could Reach $1 Billion, Mayor Says. *The SandPaper*. Retrieved from http://thesandpaper.villagesoup.com/p/long-beach-island-damage-could-reach-1-billion-mayor-says/919035

Lassonde, V.. (2012, December 13). Jetty+Waves for Water Strengthen Combined Forces for LBI's Future. *The SandPaper*. Retrieved from http://thesandpaper.villagesoup.com/p/jetty-waves-for-water-strengthen-combined-forces-for-lbi-s-future/936297

Mann, J. (2012, October 28). Sunday, October 28, 2012: Kinda quietish, though the first heavier rain bands have arrived (5:15) [Web Log Post]. www.jaymanntoday.ning.com. Retrieved from http://jaymanntoday.ning.com/profiles/blogs/715176:BlogPost:98156

_____. (2012, November 13). Sunday, October 28, 2012: Some day-after Holgate shots. [Web Log Post]. www.jaymanntoday.ning.com. Retrieved from http://jaymanntoday.ning.com/profiles/blogs/some-day-after-holgate-shots

Molinaro, M. (2012, November 5). Causeway Checkpoint Temporarily Disbanded Due to Intense Traffic During Limited LBI Reopening. *The SandPaper*. Retrieved from http://thesandpaper.villagesoup.com/p/causeway-checkpoint-temporarily-disbanded-due-to-intense-traffic-during-limited-lbi-reopening/920108#.UaVoDBwoKzY

Platt, C. (2012, November 15). Holgate Residents Allowed to Return to LBI This Weekend. *Barnegat-Manahawkin Patch*. Retrieved July 1, 2013 from http://barnegat-manahawkin.patch.com/groups/politics-and-elections/p/holgate-residents-allowed-to-return-to-lbi-this-weekend

Roberts, N. (2012, November). Ghastly Dawn – The First Week. *The Beachcomber*. Retrieved from http://thesandpaper.villagesoup.com/p/ghastly-dawn-the-first-week/1026861

Smith, D./Staff (2012, October 26). New Jersey Prepares for Hurricane Sandy's Worst. NorthJersey.com. Retrieved from http://www.northjersey.com/news/bergen/New_Jersey_prepares_for_Hurricane_Sandys_worst.html

State of New Jersey. Office of the Governor. (October 27, 2012). Governor Chris Christie and Lt. Governor Kim Guadagno meet with Office of Emergency Management, cabinet members and senior staff in preparation of Hurricane Sandy at the Regional Operations Intelligence Center (ROIC) in West Trenton, N.J. on Saturday, Oct. 27, 2012. (Governor's Office/Tim Larsen) Retrieved April 20, 2013 from http://www.state.nj.us/governor/media/photos/2012/20121027a.shtml

Sudduth, M. (2012, October 22). *A storm for the ages? Perhaps. First, it is a Caribbean concern*. www.HurricaneTrack.com [web log post]. Retrieved April 21, 2013, from http://hurricanetrack.com/2012/10/22/a-storm-for-the-ages-perhaps-first-it-is-a-caribbean-concern/

United States. National Aeronautics and Space Administration. (October 22 – November 9, 2012). *Missions – Hurricanes - Archives – Sandy*. Retrieved March 27, 2013 from the NASA Web Site: http://www.nasa.gov/mission_pages/hurricanes/archives/2012/h2012_Sandy.html

United States. FEMA. (2012, November). National Guard at Long Beach Island (video). Retrieved June 20, 2013 from http://www.fema.gov/medialibrary/media_records/10452

Venturatwenty (December 30, 2012). Firefighters Wild Response Hurricane Sandy w/ Governor, Police Military, Volunteers Surf City LBI. Retrieved June 10, 2012 from http://www.youtube.com/watch?v=XUPZN1r7xq8.

Weaver, D. (2012, November 15). Ship Bottom rescue efforts during Hurricane Sandy were like scenes out of a disaster movie. *The Press of Atlantic City*. Retrieved from http://www.pressofatlanticcity.com/news/breaking/ship-bottom-rescue-efforts-during-hurricane-sandy-were-like-scenes/article_fa371c16-2f83-11e2-9a1b-0019bb2963f4.html?mode=jqm_gal#&ui-state=dialog

Efforts to rebuild the dunes (above, in Harvey Cedars), to clear the streets of sand, and to control natural gas leaks began immediately after the storm.

Acknowledgments

Superstorm Sandy was a complex storm that left a great amount of destruction and heartbreak in its wake. The sheer number of stories from those who experienced Sandy firsthand could fill volumes. Bringing some of those stories to you in this book was no small undertaking and I would like to thank those who made it happen.

First, my editor Steve Warren worked tirelessly to help structure the book and trim and polish my words to make them the best they could possibly be. This book would not be what it is without Steve. I owe an immense amount of gratitude to him for his patience, tutelage and tremendous focus. He kept me on track, even when I didn't think I could round the bend at times. Thank you, Steve.

Part of the research for this book was a collaborative effort with Andrew Pearson and Corinne Gray Ruff, the director and producer, respectively, of the documentary film *Landfall: The Eyes of Sandy*. Some of the accounts included here came directly from recorded interviews Pearson and Ruff conducted in the research and production of their film. The three of us also worked in tandem on several interviews relating to our individual projects. We shared information and contacts, and this openness made both projects better. Not only do I feel like I met two consummate professionals in the field, I also feel like I made new friends. I owe a great many thanks to each of them.

In 1993 my mother bought *Great Storms of the Jersey Shore* from a Beach Haven bookstore and proceeded to chase down Senator Bill Bradley on his annual beach walk to get him sign it. Bradley wrote the foreword to that book and he signed, *To Scott - Best wishes from a fan of the Jersey Shore*, right above it. My mom then gave it to me as a gift. I read that book. I studied that book. I had always been mesmerized by Long Beach Island's illustrious storm history, especially the '62 Storm, which floated my parent's Holgate home across the street. Captivating stuff.

Almost a decade later I had the fortune of working with the authors of *Great Storms*, Larry Savadove and Margaret Thomas Buchholz, while a writer for *The Beachcomber* and *The SandPaper*. At 25, I was star struck. Here I was working alongside two of my favorite authors. I was green, both with envy at their tremendous writing skill, and as a rookie journalist. I learned a great deal from them both.

Flash forward another decade and here I am writing a book about Superstorm Sandy, picking up where *Great Storms of the Jersey Shore* left off. When it came time to ask renowned figures for a foreword I had in mind only two people I hoped would agree. They did. I am deeply honored to have both Larry Savadove and Margaret Thomas Buchholz play a part in this book. I express humble and sincere thanks to them for writing a foreword and an introduction to this book. As for my original copy of *Great Storms* — it sat right beside me as I wrote every chapter of *Surviving Sandy*.

Thank you to Ray Fisk and Down The Shore Publishing for approaching me with

on the phone, while others shared their accounts in interviews with Pearson and Ruff. Your stories *are* this book. These stories are part of Southern Ocean County's written history now. Even if your story isn't in print on these pages, rest assured that your participation helped bring life to the book in other ways. So thank you to all of the following (in no particular order):

Government: Mayor James Mancini, Commissioner Joseph Lattanzi and Long Beach Township, Mayor Bill Huelsenbeck and Ship Bottom Borough, Beach Haven Borough, Mayor John Oldham and Harvey Cedars Borough, Mayor Kirk Larson and Barnegat Light Borough, Borough of Surf City, Mayor Buck Evans and Tuckerton Borough, Mayor John Spodofora and Stafford Township.

First Responders: Ric Anastasi, Stanley Markoski III, and the Beach Haven Volunteer Fire Company & Water Rescue Team, Peter Hartney, Judi Hartney, Surf City Volunteer Fire Department and EMS, Chief Brian Stasik and the Surf City Fire and EMS, Barnegat Light Volunteer Fire Company, High Point Volunteer Fire Company and Chief Sean Marti, The Ship Bottom Volunteer Fire Company, Long Beach Township Police Lieutenant Paul Vereb, Long Beach Township Police Officer Patrick Mazzella, Ship Bottom Patrolmen Brian Tretola and Ronald Holloway, Ship Bottom Police Sergeant Scott Barr, and the New Jersey National Guard.

Citizens and Businesses: Jim Mahoney and family, Jack Bushko and everyone at Island Surf & Sail; Steve DiPietro and family and everyone at the California Grill; Mark Cohen and family and everyone at the Chicken or the Egg; Rick Schmid, David Schmid and everyone at Dutchman's Brauhaus; Joseph Rulli and everyone at Joey's Pizza and Pasta; Jon Coen; Curt and Gail Travers, Jay Mann, Pat Johnson, and everyone at *The SandPaper*; Deborah Whitcraft, Skip, Trisha, and Patrick Carey (and family friend Brandon), Carl & Susan Clark, Marilyn & Buzz Howard, Ron and Barbara Wilson, Don and Clarice Kartan, Sandy Gingras, the Bowker Family, Andrew Warren and family, Dave and Cindy Wood, Lloyd Vosseller and family, Ashley Vosseller, Charlie Potter and family, Dr. Joseph Lattanzi and Dr. Kim Hogan, Zach Kerzner and Ruby Red Dog and everyone at Acme Surf and Skate; the Perry family; Pete Pianetti, Randy Townsend; Jeremy DeFilippis, Corey Higgins and everyone at Jetty; Rick McDonough, Brian Farias, Brian Cohen, Joe Mangino, Chris Huch; Angela Andersen and family; Chris Pollillo, Gerard Schultz, Ron Ronolson, Ed and Marie Hoffman, Shawn and Debbie Murphy at D & S Marina, Dawn Giovannoli and family, Dennis and Jill Belloff, Wendy and Mike McCrann, Jimmy Ward, Fr. Steven Kluge; Tom Hughes and everyone at the Sea Shell Motel; Diane Frey and everyone at Fantasy Island; the

this book idea and allowing me the opportunity to work with you to create a document of the Sandy experience. A little idea grew into a substantial project. I am proud to have a title within the list of your extensive catalogue.

Special thanks to Leslee Ganss, who made this book look as amazing as it does. I appreciate all the guidance and support from both Ray and Leslee throughout the project. Proofreader Kathy Whartenby also deserves special thanks; I know she had her work cut out for her.

Everyone whose stories line these pages deserves a thank you. I met some of you personally or the Hillman family and everyone at the Engleside Inn, David Kaltenbach; Scott Russo, Joe Wright and everyone at ScoJo's, Joann Cohalan and family, Art Levy and Abhi Taranath of Holgate Update — thank you to everyone who shared on social media through Holgate Update — and LBI Trailer Park.

Science: Gary Szatkowski of the National Weather Service in Mount Holly, NJ, Dr. Stewart Farrell and Dan Barone of the Coastal Research Center at Stockton College.

Finally, I thank my family for all of their patience and unwavering support during this project. It's hard enough dealing with a husband and father who is an educator and brings a lot of work home. Add all the time for researching, writing and revising a book and, well, you get the idea. I could not write this book if I didn't have such a strong supportive wife and such amazing, understanding children. Thank you to my mother and father, also, for all of their support and encouragement all these years. And thank you Mom, for buying me *Great Storms* all those years ago. Who knew this is where it would lead.

At Engleside Avenue in Beach Haven a free Thanksgiving dinner was offered on the street (above). Residents line up for the "grab-and-go" day on Route 72 in Manahawkin (right). Facing page: Debris on Mayetta Landing Road, Stafford Township, the morning after the storm.

Photograph Credits

/n this digital era of social media and cameras in every cell phone, the sheer number of images of Superstorm Sandy captured and shared is unprecedented. Residents, officials, first responders, public works crews and business owners posted and shared pictures on Facebook, Twitter, Instagram, and in group emails. Many people passed around flash drives and cards to share with others, and those images were in turn copied and shared again.

The sharing of images during and after the storm was an amazing community experience — a granting of access to the events in the heart of the storm; much of this unfolded through social media.

This sharing also resulted in a great deal of mixing of content as files were copied again and again. As a result the names of the original photographers and sources may be lost. We undertook a major effort to find, organize, select, and identify the images for this book. We've done our best to identify photographers wherever we can, and they are credited below. We also know that many of the people thanked in the acknowledgments above also deserve credit for freely providing images. Thanks to all of you for making this document of the storm complete, and if your image is not credited, you are thanked nonetheless for contributing to this history.

Special thanks to the intrepid photojournalists and staff at *The SandPaper* (who managed to produce a newspaper immediately after the storm, without missing a beat, when their office was inaccessible and the Island was off-limits), in particular to Photo Editor Ryan Morrill, photojournalist Jack Reynolds, and Managing Editor Jay Mann. Also, special thanks to former Beach Haven Mayor and New Jersey Maritime History Museum founder Deb Whitcraft for providing thousands of images we sorted through; to photographer Ashley Vosseller-Smith for her excellent work documenting the storm and access to her files; to Andy Warren of the Surf City Public Works Department; and to all of you who mailed and emailed us photographs.

Ric Anastasi: 42 (both), 67, 82, 131 (top right), 177, 178. **Travis Cain:** 30 (left)
Tricia Carey: 99 (top). **Carl Clark:** 59, 61, 94 (top right), 98, 99 (bottom), 100 (top), 101, 106 (left), 128 (bottom). **Ray Fisk:** 28, 31, 69, 70, 71, 72, 76, 77, 104 (top left; bottom right), 106 (right), 108 (top left; top right; bottom right), 109 (both), 110, 111, 122 (top), 136, 138 (left), 139 (top right; bottom right), 141 (left), 145 (right; bottom left), 147 (top), 149 (right), 151 (right), 152 (all), 153 (both), 154 (bottom right), 155, 156, 159 (right), 162 (right), 164 (bottom right), 165 (top left), 166 (bottom), 172, 175, 179, 184. **Leslee Ganss:** 141 (right), 160, 164 (top left; bottom left), 166 (top), 167 (left), 180.
Sandy Gingras: 104 (bottom left). **Harvey Cedars Police Department:** 9, 24, 30 (right), 32 (bottom), 33, 45, 53 (left), 54, 62, 100 (bottom left), 123 (top left, top right, bottom right), 124 (bottom left), 131 (bottom right), 137 (right), 170, 174, 176. **High Point Volunteer Fire Company:** 25, 29, 32 (top), 120. **ISRO/NASA/JPL-Caltech:** 21. **Don and Clarice Kartan:** 37, 63, 116. **Jay Mann/** *The SandPaper:* 36, 64, 112, 113. **Michael Molinaro/***The SandPaper:* 121. **Ryan Morrill/** *The SandPaper:* 17, 23 (right) 27, 55, 56, 81 (top), 86,87,88, 91, 92, 94 (bottom right), 95, 102, 114, 115, 119, 123 (bottom left), 124 (top left), 127 (top; right), 130 (all), 131 (top right), 132 (both), 137 (left), 148, 150, 151 (top), 161, 162 (left), 171, 175 (bottom left). **NASA:** 38. *NASA GOES Project:* 14, 20. **Jack Reynolds/***The SandPaper:* 35, 78, 128 (top), 129 (both), 142 (left; bottom right), 143 (all), 144, 145 (top left), 165 (bottom). **Robert Rue:** 73, 74 (both), 75, 159 (bottom left; bottom right). *The SandPaper:* 26, 43 (right), 44 (right), 51 (right), 52 (right), 53 (right), 60, 78, 80, 83, 84 (bottom left; top left), 91 (bottom right), 117, 118, 126, 131 (bottom left), 135 (top), 163 (top; bottom), 164 (top right), 147 (bottom), 165 (top right), 167 (right). **Ashley Vosseller-Smith:** 103, 125, 127 (bottom left), 134, 140, 168. **John Tomaro:** 126 (left; bottom right). **US Army Corps of Engineers:** 13. **US Coast Guard:** 90. **Andy Warren:** 2, 7, 10, 22, 32, 34, 40, 41, 47, 55, 56, 57, 65, 81 (bottom), 84 (bottom right), 89, 91 (top right), 93 (right), 96, 97, 100 (right), 107, 175, 178, 181, 183. **Deb Whitcraft:** 49, 51 (left), 52 (left).

Index

*Down The Shore Publishing specializes in books, calendars, cards and videos about
Long Beach Island and the Jersey Shore. For a free catalog of all our titles or to
be included on our mailing list, just send us a request:*

Down The Shore Publishing
Box 100, West Creek, NJ 08092

info@down-the-shore.com
www.down-the-shore.com